Stop All the Clocks

More Conversations with Shaman, Taiji
Master, Rainforest Activist

Jef Crab

Margaret A. Harrell

Following Up on *An Underground PRINCIPIA*

Praise for Margaret A. Harrell's Books
Selected Review Snippets

Space Encounters II, rev. ed.—An Underground PRINCIPIA

Margaret Harrell has the most open-ended and far-reaching mind of anyone I know."
— Rhea A. White, Director, the Exceptional Human Experience Network

"My biggest concern is that I have no idea how many people will be able to grasp the depth of the principles you describe. It is amazing enough that you take a lifetime of experiences and connect them into a driving force that leads to the realization of one's purpose. Even more amazing is that you include the most subtle levels of existence that play a role in these processes. *An Underground PRINCIPIA* connects life purpose, spirituality, depth psychology, and quantum physics into one all-encompassing movement.

"Most breathtakingly, by reading *An Underground PRINCIPIA,* the reader can gain the insight that all of this is happening, not in one lifetime, whether human or universal, but in an eternal now. Amazing achievement."
— Jef Crab, Master Taiji teacher, Shaman, rainforest activist

The *Hell's Angels* Letters: Hunter S. Thompson, Margaret Harrell and the Making of an American Classic

"Thompson's motto might well have been 'Nothing in moderation.' For *The Hell's Angels Letters*, Margaret Ann Harrell—in collaboration with Ron Whitehead—has assembled a dossier of all her correspondence with Thompson during the time she worked as the editor of the gonzo writer's 'strange and terrible saga of the outlaw motorcycle gangs.' Typed manuscript pages, scribbled notes, photographs, interviews, and all sorts of period ephemera relating to Hell's Angels allow the reader a valuable, behind-the-scenes glimpse into the making of this classic of New Journalism."

—Michael Dirda, *The Washington Post*

"Whether typed or scrawled in giant letters with a red pen, Thompson's correspondence is invariably annotated and corrected in his unique way, adding a layer of personality that was missing from the collections, as well—of course—as Harrell's explanations that provide further insight."

—David Wills, *Beatdom*

"A big book, literally and figuratively . . . A fabulous present for you, or anyone in your life who admires Thompson's numerous achievements . . . It's worth every penny. T*he Hell's Angels Letters: Hunter S Thompson, Margaret Harrell and the Making of an American Classic* gets five stars out of five! Bravo!"

—Kyle K. Mann, *Gonzo Today*

Space Encounters III, rev. ed.—*Inserting Consciousness into Collisions: A True Fantasy Adventure by the Earth through the Quantum-Entangled World*

"A wizard at turning the sign language of the specifics into messages of the beyond . . . A fantastic journey into the source of creativity. Another re-storying of how our lives are entangled in the grandiose web of the universe. This time taken from a myriad of perspectives: quantum leaps and how they shake up the Newtonian mechanistic worldview, Jungian archetypal wisdom seen from a quite unique angle, the huge impact on a life's course starting with childhood imprints, spicy poetic wordplay endowed with meaning . . . a writer who composes symphonies of words and dances along the cosmic plot lines she is detecting . . . Read this book as an eye-opener, I-opener, beyond the eye/I. Join the dance of *Space Encounters* III!"

—Chris Van de Velde, coach, teacher, and trainer, Light Looper

Stop All the Clocks

More Conversations with Shaman, Taiji Master, Rainforest Activist Jef Crab

Margaret A. Harrell

Many thanks to Dirk Gillabel for granting permission to reprint his translation of Jóska Sóos's essay on the seven spheres of consciousness and for his preservation of the paintings and text.

ISBN (hardcover): 979-8-9904800-6-3
ISBN (softcover): 979-8-9904800-7-0

Cover design and interior graphic: Deborah Perdue, https://illuminationgraphics.com

A Published in Heaven Series Book

Published in Heaven Books include titles by His Holiness The Dalai Lama, President Jimmy Carter, Thomas Merton, Seamus Heaney, Hunter S. Thompson, Jack Kerouac, Andy Warhol, Allen Ginsberg, Yoko Ono, William S. Burroughs, Edvard Munch, Diane di Prima, Jim Carroll, Amiri Baraka, Gregory Corso, John Updike, Rita Dove, Wendell Berry, David Amram, Douglas Brinkley, BONO, Ron Whitehead, Lawrence Ferlinghetti, and many more.
Published in conjunction with Saeculum University Press of Sibiu, Romania and Raleigh, North Carolina

For inquiries, signed copies, and speaking requests, contact
marharrell@hotmail.com
https://margaretharrell.com

To all my energy friends, mentioned and unmentioned
And my friends who incarnated those energies
And came to share this time with me

Contents

Recognize that you're bringing together elements. And what's going to matter most as you bring those elements together is your experiential way of holding that energy. To the degree that you can form an assistance by an intellectual picture or a sort of mental picture of what these energies are, that's fine. But if you find that your mental picture and your experience aren't quite matching, always go with experience. Always. The experience has the power to take you to these places your intellectual picture never will. But, on the other hand, make sure that you get enough mental picture to support you doing it.

—Duane Packer

You can't *make* your life happen. You have to be ready for it, build up to it—let seeds grow.

Luck is a very thin wire between survival and disaster, and not many people can keep their balance on it.

—Hunter S. Thompson

My biggest concern is that I have no idea how many people will be able to grasp the depth of the principles you describe. It is amazing enough that you take a lifetime of experiences and connect them into a driving force that leads to the realization of one's purpose. Even more amazing is that you include the most subtle levels of existence that play a role in these processes. *An Underground PRINCIPIA* connects life purpose, spirituality, depth psychology, and quantum physics into one all-encompassing movement.

Most breathtakingly, by reading *An Underground PRINCIPIA*, the reader can gain the insight that all of this is happening, not in one lifetime, whether human or universal, but in an eternal now. Amazing achievement.

—Jef Crab, *An Underground PRINCIPIA* review

I'm not a proponent of making my life difficult.

—Jef Crab

Life is my hobby.

—Jef Crab

Consciousness wins every time.

It will drive things to the surface.

It waits. It says:

Now!

"Gentlemen, this case is absolutely unique—tomorrow we shall have another just like it."

—Carl Jung

Author's Note

After Jef made his comment on the unlikelihood of many people "grasping the depth of the principles you describe" in *An Underground PRINCIPIA*, we decided—by sheer happenstance—to do something about it. The decision "just materialized," as if decided for us. Consciousness, as I said, drove The Next Step to the surface.

In this new book you will find some demonstrations of the consciousness the *Principia* is operating in—explication, as well. It's stepped down, even stepped "up." As Jef puts it, "I'll be very specific about some of my experiences. But now I see it's about *incarnating* the energy. And what I take it to be—it is this domino: you actually push one and then a whole new section is falling down, but actually it's opening up."

This book takes off from my *Principia*, not Newton's, though who knows his unstated thoughts because there were so many veils back then over what he questioned, what raised his suspicions. From different corners of the Earth, *Stop All the Clocks* has ferreted out answers that were not so accessible in Newton's day and after, but that we need the lived wisdom of now. It happened organically. We had a few Zoom chats. As always, with Jef, these talks go deep. I easily realized they were taking us somewhere that others would want to go to. And inserting themselves into my new manuscript. I hadn't known where the barely begun—but zooming along as on a speed track—manuscript was going. Like always, I just started and curiously waited to see what next. There was a lot of empty space. And these chats just dropped in. I was relieved that suddenly the *Principia* material became much much more "digestible." Jef being highly motivated, he wrote me:

Hi, Margaret,

This morning I had an insight after practicing Taiji and doing a little meditation—that I would like to compare the situation we find ourselves in today to those gigantic structures consisting of hundreds of thousands of dominoes. These structures typically comprise various layers and regions, where each addition to the overall setup naturally requires one domino to initiate the movement of the structure.

For me, *An Underground PRINCIPIA* is one of those dominoes that will cause an entire structure to collapse. It is evident that we are living in a time where a paradigm shift is occurring: the narrative we have used so far is no longer valid. It only tells us about economic and financial structures as a salvific model. Heck, it is not even a science, like quantum physics or biology, but merely a set of assumptions and ever-changing rules. Only a few, it should be noted, determine these rules—to their advantage.

So this *narrative*, which is imposed on almost everyone, says nothing about who or what we are, what we are doing here, or what the proper relationship with our environment should be.

The recent flood in Valencia—my brother is living there—which claimed over a hundred lives, is a clear sign that we have understood little or nothing about how the processes on this planet function. *Naming* what happens, labeling an event, is certainly not a sign or proof of that insight. If we truly understood the processes within ourselves and in the world, we would not find ourselves in the current situation.

The only thing we can do is remain open to the new narrative when it presents itself as the old one crumbles. Books like *An Underground PRINCIPIA*—and probably this one we are writing together—can help us recognize it. The paradigm shift is happening anyway, whether we like it or not.

So naturally, I was all ears to see what the Universe had to say. Sometimes through Jef, sometimes directly to me. Where was the earth going?

Here goes.

Part One

Chapter One

Stop all the clocks, cut off the telephone,
Prevent the dog from barking with a juicy bone,
Silence the pianos and with muffled drum
Bring out the coffin, let the mourners come.

Let aeroplanes circle moaning overhead
Scribbling on the sky the message "He is Dead."
Put crepe bows round the white necks of the public doves,
Let the traffic policemen wear black cotton gloves.

—W. H. Auden

This story is about being snatched from death—literally.

Being snatched from its jaws, from its clutches. Just at the life-threatening moment. But the rescue "mechanism" went back decades. Let me tell you.

With eyes closed, I was meditating in a light body journey. The idea was to look at your own death. Suddenly I saw a timeline with an obstacle on it: an end point. Anything beyond that was blocked from access. So that was IT. The moment. A barrier. Impassible.

But no. Hands started piling gifts in front of the end point, preventing it from being An Ending that went without remark. From happening with silence and lack of input. Pushing it further back. Just as if somewhere there was recognition:

> Earth, receive an honoured guest:
> William Yeats is laid to rest.
> Let the Irish vessel lie
> Emptied of its poetry.
>
> —Auden

Or was it Dylan Thomas, "Do not go gentle into that good night"? What patterns stepped up: don't go on *as if* nothing extraordinary has happened?

Not *removing the stone from a grave and letting the inhabitant out, after death*—no, this was not that pattern.

But one just preceding it, cutting it off, cutting death off, with presents and solemnity brought by unknown events and people, as in a celebration. But that's a pattern too. I recognize it. Wisemen bringing gifts.

My heart surged. They were indicating joy and appreciation, *not* letting what had looked like a final moment proceed—emissaries in a block interceding. At least not letting the moment occur unremarked on, delaying it. How long? The picture didn't show me that. Maybe saying: *It's up to you. Do you want to make something of this delay? Your life or death depend on it.* As if there had been a collapse—particlely speaking—a rising up—of the straight-ahead line of approach, one that must have been, in some map, a "plan." A prediction.

Who (or what) *perused the map* and thought: *No?*

Which reminds me of the guru I saw, his eyes falling with intent on a photo of his devotees. I was aware, as I recounted in telling the story in *An Underground PRINCIPIA*,

3

that—in casting his eyes over the faces—he was transmitting energy to them individually. It was clearly the case. At least, to me. Merely by a look, he was—at a distance—"sending" them a "packet" of energy. Individually.

This vision of delay at the thought-to-be tomb was as if someone perused my life, my image, just like that and said: *Here's energy to rewrite the would-be end, put time on a different track, steer the train onto it at the determined-to-be final moment. It's a chance. Will she take it?*

They looked so solemn. They knew I would. Did not doubt the outcome. Doubt would have been deadly.

And who/what set in motion this attempt to waylay death, like a highwayman at a stagecoach, to put a positive karma if you will—a different outcome, at least temporarily—in its path? A switch of the briefcase as one runner passed another. To waylay it with another pattern. You don't think such a thing is possible? Well, I'm telling you it is.

I am calling it the Wisemen Bringing Gifts at the Birth of Christ. The initial pattern, or event, now seen as pushed aside by a different pattern. But hold on, it was a death pattern I saw. What had it to do with wisemen? Yes, I know you are asking if patterns can become Lego blocks that you build with, puzzle pieces you move into a new end result. Chess pieces on some very high energetic level where Form creates with the past—or everything at its disposal.

Yes! I already posited that. Whoever read my last book (anyone? Speak up) is a tiny bit familiar with the idea. I gave a few examples but barely broke the ice on the topic. It was just my word (and experience and channeled messages: my consciousness, that is) against the Earth consciousness, the Establishment, which as of yet didn't know it existed, as it didn't know about many other practices we live inside that surely exist and affect us.

4

This vision of my grave—not the artificial-flower/vase type, but a real tombstone, sitting solitarily—all at once, almost the instant I saw the vision, it was reversed: but it depicted itself to me long in advance of any real life threat: over a decade earlier. It promised that at such a day in the future, when I was threatened by death, some people would show just how much they cared, come out of the woodwork to do it. When? The depiction took place in no time frame. Just a tomb that was not—yet—to hold a deceased person, me. I *didn't* get into it. There was a Halt! Stop. Blessings first. *Blessings that seemed to replicate an entirely different pattern. To the rescue.*

And after the blessings—?

Well, that's NOW.

At least a decade ago, this future was locking itself into place *as an option*. Now, if you don't believe that's possible, keep reading and just follow the facts. You can even apply them to yourself.

So, today, at 11:49 a.m. September 27, 2024, a couple of days after my eighty-fourth birthday (yes, so ancient), I had no plan to go back into this text. But I woke with a fluttering on my eyelids. I just wrote a poem describing why.

> Did I make the right decision? I asked
> Canceling events
> Was that isolating me
> Cutting me off from the energy that kept me pointed toward
> the Light pole that stalked the sky, looking for
> Likeness
>
> Waking, I felt flutters beneath my lids

Flutters that joined me as I woke,
Barely noticeable
energy, a vibration
Near
At the computer a great surprise awaited
The sparkle beings
this time on my left side.
there they were.
They knew things
I'm to be present for

They
blind me from seeing some of what's on the computer
made of light
Am I one of them
Old gurus wanted to turn into light
I almost melt into the sparkle beings

I cannot see outside them
even down at my left hand
almost—yes—on my wrist like a watch
I see them, moving as my hand
types
As the typing sets up an alignment
With I know not what except it's their work

Just stay and wait
for
Words

My eyes
fill with light

I cannot see, almost
staring at the screen, and the light, the wave motion,
of the
Sparkle beings is there
also in my awareness
Focused on their vibrating, tinsel-like presence
pointedly
Sheets of
Color
Fluttering in places so fast it
is a state of mind they create, not the sense of going
anywhere
But of being somewhere
Many places, one place
No place, where consciousness comes from, is, aware
burrowing deeper
there. Where they also are

My decision did not strike them as wrong
their presence tells me
And they will also come to me to reinforce what I'm
doing
What is that?
I am sitting in an energy field
And they are supporting the field
Helping me locate it
I know nothing of
What to
Do
Next
What's coming
Where I'll be needed

My time, years

Here
Where they are
Bringing
Tinsel-like light fields
That pass and stop with energy, joy, delight, wonder
Put me into the field
of light
Make my heart flutter
Merging with
them
Remind me of
our connection which
I
Know
Not
Except the Light they convoy
Conveys

The vision—from no later than 2010—of the presents being piled in front of what had otherwise been my death, my grave, winged its way out of abstraction, out of No Time, out of probability, into my life concretely, factually, direly, in 2022, with my diagnosis with breast cancer. I have rarely put this into print before. I mentioned illness but not the name.

I remembered the vision, of course, almost instantly, upon hearing the diagnosis. And suddenly, while I dived into as much creativity as possible, as much gratitude for my life, people now came to assist—(many did not know that I now had no hair at all, wore a wig)—startling me as just in their kindness, upbeatness, they joined in my healing.

So the Alpha–Omega, which I've referred to before—this time, though, being for the first time, starting at "Bringing gifts"—at a birth—skips right to The End. But what's the end? *No*, said the Omega. *Merge the two*, and the Beginning rebegins, pushing The End aside, playing "Musical Chairs." Dashing the hopes of The End to slip itself in.

For here—revising, moving the LEGO blocks around—the somber, serious-looking group stood in my vision at what would be the grave, but it's not that: the empty grave, though in this case, the displaced grave, the non-grave, the moved-back grave, is not allowed into this *Now*. It's the location of gifts, tangentially—or critically?—in a side slant. As if in its energetic world, the two past events, the Wisemen's visit and the Resurrection, could be moved side by side and all the meaning of one event be emptied into the other, sliding it out, stepping into its position. Cross-pollinating in our world.

Could all events be moved around this way?

I am saying so. But let's go on.

Today I slip another piece in place, connect another otherwise-far-apart event.

In 2022, while recalling this meditation—the one with the intercepted end—but making no connection with the co-founder of my light body/luminous body work, *who had led that very meditation years before*, I told him about my illness; I was in the Seed Group and felt he should know. I didn't expect more than a passing response. Of course, he knew nothing about my meditation above.

But what he sent back was the message he'd set up a "healing path of pure Light." For me to walk on, he said. Now my assignment became to merely walk on "a path of pure Light." That, with traditional medication, was "the cure.

Find it. If I could. I was convinced.

Immediately, I set this as my priority.

Never did it leave my mind. I felt my life depended on it. That and an outlook of joy and gratitude that automatically descended on me.

"But Duane doesn't do personal things," someone said, meaning the light body co-founder. True. I knew it. Nevertheless, timing of the vision was activated.

Gifts, not wailing, surrounded me. I wrote and wrote and wrote, rescuing manuscripts put aside decades ago that had been "brought to me" to steward by "spirit committees" during a ten-year stay alone in Belgium.

And only today I realize the connection between the vision of the interception of Death in the DaBen seminar—years ago as Duane channeled DaBen—and the Path of Pure Light set up by Duane when the vision entered "reality," in 2022. I stop to digest it, dumbfounded.

How Time was doing flip-flips. I had sensed back then the energized visual was "real"—that outside linear time I was seeing a scene from the future clairvoyantly. Sensing even then that it could (and did) get a foothold (in 2022) and become—? The promise foretold. I had a huge sense of ebullience, of reassurance, total faith the vision had reality concealed inside it. The group standing around, forestalling normal time, seemed so serious, of such stature. On such a vibration. I never forgot it.

And it stepped into Earth time. How? Off what platform in space?

But this morning I realized—wait a minute—*the path itself* must have existed back then. *Waiting for me to find it.*

Did the sparkle beings know of it, congratulate me for being on it? For they began to visit me the first day I returned home from chemo. There they were, in dancing circles around me in my hall

I did not realize the Unconscious Path, striking like a thunderbolt, had deposited itself in my mind back then. The layers all aligned: soul to physical. Why had I gotten deathly ill? *Was it to get me to look for this Path of Pure Light? Hoist me up on it?*

On one level, at least, I imagine it so—that my soul, sure I was ready for this test, had used this "travel mechanism." So I was to plunge without a net.

I had by then realized (been shown, illustrated in visions and actions) that an event could use another event as a model—as if one event could simply "clothe" itself in another. Or, put it another way, all things that happened once happened inside a "track."

We knew since at least Newton that all particles of matter in the universe were connected *to all other particles of matter*. But now I was relating that to events. Events (organized particles of matter, composed of people and objects made of matter) fell under this theory too. Didn't they? Events from different time points could—not clash, but walk into each other. Make connections. Reconstruct probability. Well, it's doubtful they could do this all on their own. But consciousness could work in them. Right?

You got it. An edge, a leg up, in reality reconstruction.

Through—?

Through consciousness reconstruction.

In this book I will sometimes engage in inner dialogue—am I talking to someone? I don't know. But the dialogue does just jump in, unannounced.

An event (depending on matter to take place in) could use a former event as "particles of matter" to steer itself away from imminent peril or error. That's the premise, and I'd seen a guide working in this principle, showing it to me, all the way back to my Zurich Initiation in 1985, 1986. Again, in 1994 I saw it in a merger with and vision of Jesus trying to bring about a successful outcome (in the unconscious) by bringing two archetypes together—two highly energized historical scenes everyone is familiar with—in cross-fertilization. But still, it was a principle not known on the Earth.

Like laying two events on a map. In the last instance, in 1994, trying to overpower the negative outcome in the present with the positive outcome in the historical event. Overpower how? By the sentiment of the people exposed to the choice in the unconscious.

It was now or never, for me. I had to integrate these principles I'd been taught in that cosmic-guide initiation in Zurich. Again in Belgium. Or go to my grave, not having personally lived my lessons. Left them in Knowing, which is not 100 percent knowing, because it has not been taken into matter and stood in. Been talked about intelligently before audiences other than the audience of one, myself. And a few readers.

So now here came Jef to help me spread the mutual consciousness, at least a little. At least put it into the air to be found. Jef not in a robe of wiseman, but didn't he fit the bill? And why put these principles only into the air? Or books? No. I wanted to stand in my own ideas. Oops. My own reality. My own consciousness.

So how does this hookup of one event to another take place—to hook in with an ending it was not headed for?

The current event was, the vision showed, headed toward a particular outcome. Now declared premature. Not much chance of avoiding it, though. We assumed the result depended on physical steps, physical facts. But then, on a high subtle level, here came the rescue, or rather, a powerful event whose outlines, potency, could move the doomed event into a different outcome state. It was just as in Zurich. The guide there instructed me to turn every negative dream-ending positive. Not to analyze "what it meant" but to just—not using logic or trails of action—hop-think it mentally to a positive end.

But where did this coupling of events take place? I knew it happened; spirit entities had "showed" me their attempts to modify a current event, using an ancient high-energy event. I have written about this, but perhaps you didn't read those books. Here goes with one example: I was at an international dream conference, in a workshop of Robert Moss, who proposed to us an exercise: to allow our body to initiate a movement by itself, organically. Expecting nothing, I felt my energy "taken over"; then, as my body continued to lightly move, I "saw" two alternative scenes: on the left hand side of me, straight ahead, was Jesus, choosing disciples. I was tightly merged, or fused, with that energy and intent. It was live. On the right hand side—not live—it was around 29 AD, in Marchaerus (modern-day Jordan). Salome was dancing before King Herod for the head of John the Baptist. The live scene, the Living Energy was fighting to defeat the still-life image of the Dance of Death. The struggle relocated that night. No one the wiser, while we all slept, we were the "subjects" of a parapsychology test No one told us it was taking place. But I found myself repeatedly waking to push "Come on, baby, let the good times roll" away, in favor of "This, this is Christ the King." The two songs were opposed. Clashing. I had no idea what was going on. Nor why I chose the one over the other. I didn't yet realize it was a continuation of the pattern of Jesus selecting disciples, as opposed to the Salome dance in a plea for the beheading.

Meanwhile, unknown to me, a dancing "sender" in the parapsychological experiment was attempting to influence the attendees to choose a sexually potent image of Rumi in photographs that would be laid out on a table the next day. Which to choose was being cemented in their minds unconsciously the night before as the choice played out in the transmitted battle as they slept. Nearby, the woman designated to "send" them the desired image was energetically dancing. But the next day, the majority of the attendees went with the spiritual choice, nobody knowing a Lesson in the Unconscious was taking place. The attendees just chose the Vibration they resonated with.

The parapsychological test was deemed a failure, with no one the wiser about the higher-level interception of it, slanting it *to a different question.*

Repeatedly, I had learned about presenting choices to individuals in their unconscious.

But here did the event-to-event connection take place—in a rendezvous in space?

In pure atmospheric collision? For sure, it took place in comparative, emotion-laden images in very sharp focus. A powerful intention had set itself the task of swerving the destined outcome, using a model pattern, a prior event, that, as here, "struck" it, like a meteor, knocking it off course.

So past events that went into our awareness did not just "go out to pasture." They remained on standby.

No?

Yes, they were there to be used again.

It might even seem like it "just happened," that wishes and prayer and so on worked.

14

Which they did.

This part took place unconsciously. But I was a Herodotus of the Unconscious, it turned out. Or the Unconscious (to us) was giving me the information from, multidimensionally, its secrets, giving me the key, passing it *through* me.

One big thought like this a day, and I feel alive.

One big connection, dimension to dimension.

You can't tell me that a piling of presents before what would have been my death point was a random vision that just happened to click into my life over a decade later. And be a match.

So how does time do it—be both linear in our world? And nonlinear? How did it come up with an image, kinetic, then leave it in potential, looming but not relevant for years; then wake it up, kinetic again. There's no way it was random. No statistics expert would give you any odds. No. *It was precognitive.*

Like time was a *switch* on events, saying when to move, turned on and off and on. Or it had a switch. Like electricity, connected to time—or timeliness, when its time came— turned "on" an unsuspected subtle probability that knocked other possibility or probability out of orbit.

You tell me. Can *time conceal the future in visions in the present,* power-packed potential? Move them into storage; then on a signal they spring alive, as a piece of your life, moved from vision to kinetic matter. Because—because—now we are getting close to a truth. Or law. Because, for one thing, it had been viewed—observed, reacted to, marveled at—internally powerfully. By me. Because it was about my life. It said: *Look, there's this way to get through a life-threatening moment in time, where one outcome is death, another is presents and celebration*

15

filling it instead, swerving it off course or rather moving it onto the correct course for your next decades.

Tell me if that is not what happened.

And if I hold up a placard, can it be like a beacon to direct a future event to it?

But that's what meditating with intent is, isn't it?

That it can be a placard, what a weird thought. Weird reality. Like a lighthouse signaling to Light. Like demonstrators to the Other World, to the multiple dimensions, holding up signs *to campaign for them to come here.* To *lure* them. To energize them. Show support for them in advance. Making pictures in electricity—again we find that topic on our agenda, taken further. For sure.

So this morning by appearing to me, the sparkle beings, the Light field that I see only as a tinsel-like group of consciousness beings, identified only by their vibrating at my side at the computer, "told" me, unconsciously, to go back to this book after about six months of not picking it up. They came on a mission. They brought energy for something they cared to have me work on. They were, like always, keeping me alive by keeping me busy in a Light Field.

※

But I am not shapeless energy. The thought strikes me.

I've been saying that energy travels, is not kept inside my physical boundaries. But the thought annihilates that one.

So what? it says. *You have been telling yourself you are "a focus." That you "focus" consciousness, that the "focus" sets you apart. Sets each one who "focuses energy" apart.*

So if the energy travels, is it that the focus travels with it?

16

❋

Mulling it over:

I am not shapeless energy. My energy does not stream out without ties, alliances. It does not just go hither and thither with no stamp on it. It obeys the laws of attraction and repulsion. Right? So something *called "me"* holds onto a "focus" as it turns into pure energy?

Well, no. I wouldn't go that far.

How far would you go?

Keep typing. Keep reading.

Let's learn more about

Me, about You.

❋

So you're going to give me little bits like this—until I work up steam? Intrigue me with little sentences, thoughtful, challenging. Giving me a push to get started. Of course, that's sheer luck that you came over here to do this to me. Set me upright in my chair, my fingers on the keys, saying: *Type. All right, go ahead. Take this down and*

think about it.

"But you have a lot to live up to," I go on. "Are you going to match the books I just wrote" (I/we, whoever)?

Yes.

So I got set to see what the so-called future was laden with.

17

Talking with Jef Crab on Skype

JEF: This misinformation we get is this thing about being individual—separated from all the other things. It's difficult for us to see the connection.

You talked to me about all these glitter beings. I drew this geometric picture. [Holds up a drawing] Can you see this?

MAH: Yes, I can. It's a grid.

JEF: Actually, this grid is nothing but connected triangles. But it's in fact the structure of everything surrounding me. It has this shape, but it's all light constantly. It's vibrant all the time. Some parts of the grid are just more vivid. So they combine, they connect to each other, and they create physical forms. *They attract matter. And then something starts to exist.* But the grid is the same everywhere.

For us, it's very important that we start to look more at what is happening in the grid. And which elements are brought together—just like atoms attract each other, molecules attract each other. And then a physical form arises. So what is the shape, what is the form, which we have to bring forth?

We are very misguided by this idea of being an individual that accomplishes something. *The movement is already there.*

We are *being* moved, and we are being moved just like all these particles and atoms and molecules in the grid are being moved *in order to meet*. We are moved in order to meet once in a while and to reconnect. And to create something new.

MAH: So in the grid we have all these choices to pick out

something in the grid that connects with something else.

JEF: You *re*connect. You *re*connect. We don't pick. The grid picks us. We are not the ones picking. *We are driven to the point where we have to connect.* Just like the tree releases energetic-chemical signals into the soil. It absorbs its whole environment—*all* the light, *all* the moisture, whatever is around—*and it brings it in an energetic-chemical code into the soil by its roots*, and then the whole earth starts moving toward the tree in order to make the tree grow.

MAH: This is so important. [I gave an example of my sweet pea seeds newly planted in a pot.]

They're about an inch tall. These little ones. I talk to them. They don't know me. I'm so excited to see them push upwards.

JEF: Isn't it amazing that from this little piece of matter in this little pot there's such a huge plant that will arise.

Where does all this matter come from? It will multiply, this little seed that you planted, maybe a hundred times. So where is all this matter coming from?

MAH: *Where **is** it coming from?*

JEF: It can't be in the original pot where you planted it. And it can't be there in the original seed.

MAH: You mean, where is the matter that becomes taller, taller, taller coming from? It's growing, growing, growing, but what does that mean?

JEF: YES. And so once in a while, like Ron Whitehead, like you, like me, someday we will meet because we have to come together, and we have to become *larger*, we have to grow. But what does it mean exactly?

MAH: For instance, if "the crow" has a big, huge field and we think the crow is just a tiny bird, but there's a big crow field, and somehow Ron [Whitehead] gets into the field as a child, as he did and you get into the field as a child, as you did, and [later] you come together, the crow field becomes something totally different. I don't know what. But I think your manuscript "The White Crow" is fascinating . . .

It's so uncanny about Ron and that crow.

JEF: Even from the past, in the future, things have to come together. People from all different sides [of the field] . . . Something is expressing itself through this encounter. Something new is coming out of it.

MAH: Regarding why "The White Crow" had to wait as a manuscript . . . , what would you have done with it before? There was no way to publish it. Now it's got more options and you're there to take advantage of its options.

JEF: I salute the energy. This is the way I experience life. Life is happening. And actually we should lean back a little bit and observe very well. And then just take part. Whenever we have to take part, take part. If you don't have to partake, just lean back and observe. It will happen anyway.

[describes growing up in a hamlet; is now sitting in his

20

parental birth house] . . .

I'm so amazed by *An Underground PRINCIPIA*. There is so much that agrees with my own life.

[There were only eight farmhouses, and his mother was partly gypsy, from East Germany. Her father was a Roma, a gypsy].

MAH: So you are part gypsy.

JEF: One quarter. She had a lot of dreams. She was clairvoyant. She did a lot of things with herbs. She was using these Tarot cards. And the neighbors were suspicious.

The tales of my life I describe in "The White Crow" are an experiment in *An Underground PRINCIPIA*. And we agree that synchronicity is not always immediate. *The moment we can accept that even synchronicity can go back into the past, the only thing we have to do is connect the dots.*

MAH: Yes. The connection was always there. [Before I could ask the question hanging on my lips, he went on to answer it.]

JEF: And this is the core of *An Underground PRINCIPIA*. Something is already there. It's happening. But if you go into this vast energetic structure, you will see that elements come together. And we are connecting these things popping up. Even if it's in the past, the future, in nowadays words, it doesn't matter. We connect them.

There's a distinct, profound feeling: *This is important for our humanity.* And our growth. This is where the whole earth goes into the tree. The tree sends out a signal and the whole earth goes toward the tree. So these moments where we connect these dots from the past, from the future, from the now, and this understanding beyond words, beyond time—this is when the earth moves into the tree. The same things happens to human beings.

MAH: And the planet earth too.

JEF: The whole earth. It's the dream of Mother Earth. In Istanbul, if you sit there next to the Hagia Sophia—you don't have to go inside—if you sit outside, you can see the dream of Mother Earth because it is the oldest sacred place of that region. It's not a church. It's much older than Christianity and Islam and all the things around. This is a sacred place of the Earth, the Hagia Sophia.

MAH: Was it—I don't want to say "pagan" exactly?

JEF: It was before pagan. It has nothing to do with these things. The energy was always there. I experienced it also when I had the privilege to go to Stonehenge, for example. The Hagia Sophia is in direct connection to the dream of Mother Earth. It really brings you down into this Black Light. This deep Black Light from the Earth. Actually, the same thing that was on the other side of the Big Bang. It's the same dream. Something dreamed the Big Bang. This state of being manifests itself as the deepest layer of Mother Earth. The Hagia Sophia is actually expanding it there.

MAH: Jef, you said you made the movement of the clouds stop, you made time stop in your mind as a boy at school.

JEF: I just entered this state of being. I wasn't observative enough to know what was happening inside. I just entered this state of being. For some reason. At a certain time when I started to do Buddhist meditations, martial arts, I learned that there is a split between two impressions. This is the bardo: *this* is manifested, *this* is not manifested. Whenever we enter between this bardo, manifestation stops, time stops. This is also where you can enter the Hagia Sophia state of mind because the energy has probably been there since the beginning of the earth because it's so strong there. It's not eternal. We don't have a word for it.

MAH: Without time.

JEF: There is no time. Whenever I enter this state of mind when I sit between certain impressions—whenever I make a follow-up between impressions—whenever I can go deeper into this state of being, when I go into a certain bardo—it's timeless, there is no time. It's without time. And then, now I know that the clouds will stop. But do they really stop? I don't know. To the person who is in this superficial state of the manifestation, probably the clouds will just continue.

[He requests that I stop the recording so he can tell a very personal story. I will see if I can get him to change his mind. But for now this is private. I'll try hard to get him to tell you.]

Chapter Two

You had already told me this morning who I had been channeling, which I can't reveal. Not yet, anyway, if ever. Off to the eternal records.

The Earth Stimulators. I will call you that: Earth Stimulators. Or should I just say Teachers. Teaching me to teach you.

Ah, posh. You're a teacher too. Don't knock it.

And so I settled into Conversations with Me, Myself, AND THEM.

So. Hello, vacuum, are you the place that our to-be-reality is stored, hiding in visions that may give us advance notice, as the one above did? But that required human observation—? *Now, wait a minute. Who dreams?* The *New Scientist* vastly widens the scope.

ONE autumn day in 2020, Daniela Rößler drove home with a car full of jumping spiders. Her lab was closed due to covid-19 regulations, so, after a day in a dry field spent corralling her specimens, Rößler had no option other than to bring them back to her house. When, by chance, she checked on them that night, the spiders were dangling by threads of silk. "I had never seen this before," says Rößler, a behavioural ecologist at the University of Konstanz in Germany, who soon went back to the field with her colleagues. "We started filming them, just out of curiosity," she says.

24

They observed the same behaviour, but only at night. Stranger still, some months later, close monitoring in the lab using a night vision camera revealed not only that the spiders were twitching slightly but also that their eyes were moving. That is similar to what happens when humans dream, which raises the irresistible prospect that spiders could be dreaming too.

Jumping spiders aren't the only non-human animal in which we have recently found evidence of dream states. We are seeing hints of dreaming, and even nightmares, in species throughout the animal kingdom—from pigeons to octopuses. "If we appreciate the functions that could be connected with dreaming, it totally makes sense for animals to dream," says Rößler. And yet the question remains: do other animals dream like we do and, if so, what they are dreaming about? Figuring this out isn't easy but it is worth doing, not least because it might even help us to fathom the purpose of human dreams.

Could a dreaming animal add energy to an event it dreams of? "Receive" the particles of the event, attracted to some aspect of it—till we got interested? Or the event took place? Could events to-be hide there too—as my dog twitches his legs in the air—chasing? A squirrel. But on some other level, is it something else? Is this too far out there? Outlandish? *Aw, posh?* Could it be a purpose of anyone on the planet to "dream" up the future? For us all? Or sometimes just oneself?[1]

Vacuum energy is an underlying background energy that exists in space throughout the entire Universe. The vacuum energy is a special case of zero-point energy that relates to the quantum vacuum . . .

Quantum field theory states that all fundamental fields, such as the electromagnetic field, must be quantized at each and every point in space. (Wikipedia, vacuum energy)

Oops. Woooaaa. There it goes again, "at each and every point of space." But not even mentioning "of matter." To be a point in space means to be "quantized." Subdividable. How does this play out?

A field in physics may be envisioned as if space were filled with interconnected vibrating balls and springs, and the strength of the field is like the displacement of a ball from its rest position. The theory requires "vibrations" in, or more accurately changes in the strength of, such a field to propagate as per the appropriate wave equation for the particular field in question. The second quantization of quantum field theory requires that *each such ball–spring combination be quantized, that is, that the strength of the field be quantized at each point in space* . . . (ibid., my italics)

I stop. Well, all of us are "points" in space, right?

Someone speaks up—*I'd say I was many points in space—no?*

As you scour through
The vacuum
call it to you
The best of the best
Unwritten down
Preexistent
Springing to life and vanishing on the
to us
Instant
Writings we'll never read
Ideas never have
Till they come out to us
Out of
the
vacuum

so they marched out with cloaks of famous writers
cloaks of all sorts of names
they put on to speak through
or to
argue with
these lively sprung incarnated
thoughts
unincarnated
out of
the vacuum
fleeting there to last longer here
how they would have to
adapt to it
a life longer than
an incalculable finiteness
in their embryonic state

as they sparkled and
no one had an inkling
in the
vacuum

✖

Robert Ornstein: "The right side [of the brain] . . . seems to be specialized for the large elements of perception, the overall shapes of objects, the word shape, the information contained in the size, sounds, and intonation of words strung together" (*The Right Mind*, page 174).

We will have to look at life like that. How it—the intervention of the locked-in linearity system—might have confused us, citizens of the earth. Not that time isn't there, but that—

So I accepted the lead of the thought and let it sit, even if idly, in the text. But what was I thinking? Idly? It was on rocket fuel.

Now, this I wrote, not knowing what it meant either. But write it I did. Or my mind fused with my fingers did.

So St. Paul had got himself here. What was he going to do about it?

And, by the way, he could leave at any moment. Not being born this time with that name or even that full-fledged energy. The energy could be attracted elsewhere.

Could it?

With this much new life all around, perhaps it was a stepping stone here. Perhaps he would jump right into action and this body would not suffice. Or perhaps he would need no body, just have a better perspective in it than if only in the air as a guide. So he settled in.

Oops. I settled in. Not merging has no advantage in this moment. It's just telling the story. To experience it, only "I" will do. And so "I" now grew used to accepting the situation. It's still a rather distant "tale." But it's slowly looming into actuality. The idea that I will let this energy have space in my awareness. And even decision-making?

We'll see. Maybe you will turn the page and it's all vanished, upset, and been replaced by a direction that swooped in, seeing this one given location. Well, that meant it could come in too. Or instead of. Let's keep observing what is manifesting. And how it does it.

I, Paul, woke from sleep to tell these things.

Oh, shush. Keep your head down.

Which Paul?

Just keep quiet and let me speak. You'll see the connection:

Hearing there was a new big discussion about the components, speed, etc., of Light, now, I knew quite a lot about it, I thought. How it could *even talk*. A voice come right out of it. Sound, you see. And now, which came first, the Light itself or the sound of the Light as sound formed into words: "It is hard for you to kick against the pricks"—a phrase that came from—

> A Greek proverb, but it was also familiar to the Jews and anyone who made a living in agriculture. An ox goad was a stick with a pointed piece of iron on its tip used to prod the oxen when plowing. The farmer would prick the animal to steer it in the right direction. Sometimes the animal would rebel by kicking out at the prick, and this would result in the prick being driven even further into its flesh. In essence, the more an ox rebelled, the more it suffered. Thus, Jesus' words to Saul on the Road to Damascus: "It is hard for you to kick against the pricks."[2]

Oh, oh, forgot. I'm not supposed to be speaking yet. But I had learned, sleeping these two thousand years (in this Earth form here, that is, the one kept intact) how to project along a line of probability—taking the implications of a consciousness and standing beside it with *my own consciousness*, as could equally another do who had clarity about what was what. What was the ultimate outcome, long into the future. Was it reasonable to let the experimentation, started, continue? Or, in stopping it, mind you, call a halt to it by the simple expedient of thinking it into oblivion? Thinking of the other consciousness in a wall of light. Like flames for guards. What, then, would the parallel consciousness do? Certainly not conquer.

So in this speculative and hypothetical projectory, futures were looked at—in the present, including the twenty-first-century present. They were dimensions of the present present. So, no harm was done.

Only, the advanced consciousness, aware of the subtle energy of the other dimensions, was forced to a halt, in some of its plans. It was Mother Earth's gift to stop this. Because though the earth did not itself know these techniques, consciousnesses moving over into subtle energy did.

❋

Having written this passage in the twentieth century, putting it into a box, of course, I watched it come to life. Literally.

I took this as an entry point. The *question* existed. It had to first exist. On the human level it existed through the experience described above.

The answer DID NOT EXIST. I took this as my entry point into Earth dynamics.

But what kind of talk is this?

The kind that creates the interception of one dimension of a person with its life task in progress; of one dimension with its potential, buried in energy as under a Mount. Vesuvius.

The ashes of past lives, of past Earth comprehension as it raised its hoary head, shook its withered wisdom into new places; tried to find the relevant anchors. I found this powerful enough to put a large portion of the unused me into; i.e., the pattern of expansion had pushed me this far. Major adjustments could show me how to modulate and make comprehensible, usable, *the unused me*, which did not exist technically but did out there in "space." The me that was here more and more disgruntled, missing the speeded-up pace that existed when I, the unused me, was here on the scene, but that had to be made A place for. Space Encounters of this variety. Energy exploring the dynamics of the human self with its larger PROPORTIONS; i.e., its energy swirls. And worlds.

    I feel a chuckle. St Paul's breast fill up. *Well, this is different. Here I am, and just to sit at the computer—taking that as my task—I laugh. It's so different from having your head chopped off or fearing that at every step. Yet I see there's a real prospect of doing something important just like this. An armchair traveler, me who went on horseback and by ship, such as it existed then, through enemy territory, who relished writing letters. Ah, my letters. Communicating. Getting out the word. A danger then. No danger now. Just to get out the messages. And laugh. How odd this assignment is.*

Legions of writers
Gathered
Majestic, from the past
pens poised and inkpots and other stuff
they made lines in the sky, to guide thus by
the legions of the mind that knew how to bring

ancient sky language
alignment

Then a correction came
to tell us all
about being
_sol_ar

We are?

Yes.

Light images sailed and swam and twisted
Pictures . . . pictograms
Squinting into the space, look for latent form
A letter there
It might be
Who held onto the form of the physical body
solar light images sailed and swam and twisted
pictures making pictograms
Squinting into the space, one could look for latent form
A letter might be there
Who held onto the form of the physical body
might and might not know this
But if they didn't
now, now that wouldn't do, would it?
Being rigid

Chapter Three

The Path of Light came to see me in my sleep.

I'm watching a man speak.
I daren't, almost, try to say what the field he was in told me.

I find myself peering into a space where's he's talking
about
"the objectification of the energy"
As if *the objective* is using the energy

By itself? That is, the object has some say-so in it?

But of course the objective is using the energy
Did the energy otherwise have
an objective?
want to follow its own objective?

I hadn't got the powerful message I am being given in my
sleep
Then it strikes harder:
I get its impact.
I'm enveloped and struck down in it.
It clears
I feel like Einstein when the idea of *gravity as bent space*
came to visit

Holy crap, I say,
Gravity is affected
by intention.

Yes, we know. Go on.

Gravity is
affected by intention—That's My
TOW

The energy is much stronger than I am,
"weighing" in
making me massive
putting the intention of the energy into me
The intention to hold this
Theory

of Everything?

Intention affects quantum energy, we know.
We know its *power* of intention,
the mass, lent by the there-for-a-flicker Higgs boson

CERN Home: "You and everything around you are made
of particles. But when the universe began, no particles had
mass; they all sped around at the speed of light. Stars, planets
and life could only emerge because particles gained their mass
from a fundamental field associated with the Higgs boson.
The existence of this mass-giving field was confirmed in 2012,
when the Higgs boson particle was discovered at CERN."

What ho!

Based on that, here we go?

Based on that?
Side by side with that

Intention
And especially in the case of gravity
affects quantum energy, we know.
Subtle?
More or less. Both-and.

By intention, in my mind, I can draw two distant times or
objects together
Just by thinking it, experience it,
And that action influence matter;
influences the matter in my mind
its representation outside my mind
That then goes out with that intention
I know that. Teach it

Naturally, of course, you will say,
The intention itself has nothing to do with it
Only the mind holding the intention has
That is, if you allow even that much

But now a stronger energy comes in
One *to finish that thought*

Carrying the massive message
I never finished the thought
picked up the power of the thought,
Which was saying: *see there,*

You are experiencing how thought affects—
!!!!!
Gravity

Thought affects gravity!
Yes, just look realistically or mathematically at what you were
doing when you pulled your death
"date" to a different date,
Wiping out the you who had no accomplishments "to speak of,"
Not just changing the date but changing the you
for the one that had all these gifts,
received them
this
Collective energy
Piled in front of it—not just gifts, all wrapped up, physically
speaking, but also of thoughts,
"jobs," messages—exchanged the first scene and all it meant
For the second and all it brought with it.

Quick! Make a mathematical theory of it
What?
Put it into mathematics

I don't know how

But if a mathematician got onto this, he'd be knocked out
The energy has the whole quantum state behind it
Carrying
The message, the
worldview
Of how anyone *who can focus independently of all else*
On a word

Can put it into
Gravity
And what about actions?
Those too obey
The powerful
Energy-objectifying
Observer
*Pulling your death date to a different date, taking back the orig-
inal picture, exchanging it with a new, brimming-full picture,
do you not see that you were—first in an image—making a mew
Life Plot. Exchanging the burial plot for a Life Plot?*

Pushing the death date down the line. Do you not see that? And
why did it happen? What happened? Why?

*You observed the one event, and right in the DaBen/Duane
meditation*
someone, somewhere showed you, in the vision, it being whisked away
By whom? It didn't show that.
Just that an intention was operating in the energy of your life.
Or death.
And that strong intention was
changing it!

Was that all it took?
Holy crap again.
Here we go into a
Brand-new
Twenty-first century

Of course, many people were, in effect, practicing this art.
Eastern gurus had long practiced it in isolation. Sometimes in
public. Affecting the world that way. "At a distance."

Gravity was at work as the intention *bent* time—*bent* some moment in the future which perhaps those placing the gifts knew
—did they?
Anyway,
Without a VISIBLE warp in space

So you are saying there can be subtle warps in space.

Yea. You got it. I just did too.
Obviously if $E = mc^2$
There's a potential for physical energy, matter, to switch into subtle energy, and that it, being exchangeable, can operate as subtle energy in physical energy
Makes sense?

Well, let's say a field did it.
—*of pure Light?*
Of course
And Grace?
Yes,
Which brings in????
Love.
This was the work of

Love, of course.
Legions behind it?
Well, it could be just one if—
I know
If the Love was strong enough.

we could

step through

it.

Chapter Four

I ask Jef to pick up the story he told off camera.

JEF: I don't want to say this to the whole world, but it gives an example of time/no time . . . connected to the state of mind.

[But he's not ready to tell this private experience "on the record."]

MAH: That event you just described didn't just happen. It wasn't just out there happening *with nobody observing it. Or holding it. It was inside a mind that the force was operating.*

JEF: This is also my conclusion.

MAH: Amazing. And so a state of no time and a state of time—*or* was it a higher dimension coming in and making it appear as no time here. But the higher dimension was the key—not the no time but the higher dimension, which could come in and control our dimension . . . Suppose it could take all the energy of a scene in this dimension, hold it out to one person and no energy of this dimension be left for others to experience in this dimension because it was confiscating it, momentarily redirecting it.

[I don't give up on getting him to tell the story before the book is done. He will. But it will take some convincing. He's not there yet, but just wait a few more chapters.]

JEF: Through the years I developed this idea that all the possibilities exist already. It's just a matter *of how to switch from one dimension to another.* How to pass *through the Einstein–Rosen bridge to the other dimension.* How to go beyond the Big Bang or before the Big Bang.

And even in daily life situations it's possible to switch to another dimension. Because they exist. I'm certain they exist.

So it could be like stepping out of this dimension and entering another dimension.

[Jef is talking about worm holes (as described by *the* Einstein–Rosen bridge), predicted by the theory of general relativity; that is the connection between two distant points in space *through a shortcut.* The bridge, or tunnel, length is less than the distance between the beginning and end locations.]

MAH: To a minor degree people probably do it when they change their mental state *enough.*

JEF: Otherwise, Jesus couldn't disappear and reappear. Or Dhyanyogi or these saints if they didn't do these things. Suddenly he's gone and observes the others [while he's disappeared]

MAH: Who are you talking about?

JEF: Jesus. Disappearing from a state and reappearing again.

MAH: Right.

JEF: They couldn't find his body.

MAH: And sometimes the "appearance" is just in a vision in somebody's mind: for instance, "Sai Baba came and healed me in a dream." Or like with the ancient Greek: they would go to an Asclepius center and sleep there and say [some of them] he appeared in their sleep and cured them.

JEF: Me sitting in my parental birth house, I'm in a certain state of mind.

MAH: Of course, because if not your particles might fly apart. [Laughing] But you're very convinced you exist in this body. I guess if you were totally unconvinced, still you'd have to have a very strong mind to make it happen. But probably—maybe—some people do; they have such a strong mind that they disappear, their particles fly away.

JEF: I'm more convinced that I exist in *this* [holds up his drawing of a grid].

I also experience this physical body when I'm in that state of mind. I can reconnect with it. Or I can go into something else.

MAH: Umph.

JEF: This is a matter of directing the intention. Do I direct it to my physical presence? Or do I direct it to go deeper into this field of life and seeing the dots, and maybe going deeper into this past present future in a no-mind state of mind?

MAH: My light body teacher in Belgium works a lot with spirits. He has this massive ability to channel love and light and beauty and communicate. That's just all he is now. But he's not living in this dimension, except his body comes here. But he says things like, "If you want me to 'set the energy,' tell me what you want to happen and I'll set the energy, but I can't be involved in the logistics." I like that very much.

When my brother-in-law was dying, in hospice, one time when I went over to visit and I was bending over his bed, saying goodbye, he said, "Hans came to see me today." My sister said, "You mean *your* dog, Bonnie." And he said, "No, Hans. He came right through that bathroom door." So I went back to my house and I realized my mini-dachshund Hans had witnessed the meditations we did for my brother-in-law; he'd been sitting beside us in his dog bed. And he experienced them on his level.

While he had sat half a foot from me, I had told a class of two women, very advanced meditators, "I have to stop this meditation because there's a barrier between me and you. My mind is somewhere else."

To correct that, we meditated to send my brother-in-law energy, and I saw him *going up and down, up and down. In and out of his body, I felt sure. In and out of this dimension. And Hans was sitting there in his bed, witnessing all that.* I don't know if he went to see Richard before or afterwards.

Now [in 2024, just about a week before my birthday] my sister dropped dead. Her heart stopped, and it was all so choreographed. By happenstance, my nephew went out there to the back yard at just that moment and he saw it and can't wake her. So he called 911 and she was taken to the hospital; they didn't think they could save her. But they did. And then when she was coming out—they'd given her all these pain-killers—she had no idea what she was saying; she was way wonked out. And she didn't like the face mask, which they said she had to have. And here's the funny thing she says. She says, "You all are so naive. Richard wouldn't allow anything like that." But in a feisty language. Imitating his energy.

The only thing I could figure out was that he was there. He was so strong-minded. Forceful. I figured out he was giving that strength to her because otherwise I can't see why she would even mention him. He's been gone about seven, eight years.

JEF: When she was there, she met him.

MAH: He was giving that energy to her to fight: *come back, you don't have to die.* He pushed it into her like a shot. And she accepted it and started using it. It was beautiful. And having seen him go up and down like that and being able to communicate with Hans . . . She was really fighting, telling her son, "You're trying to kill me" (in ripping off the mask).

Talk about dimensions and being able to go back and forth. She needed to have all that fighting energy.

JEF: One day we'll better understand this.

MAH: You think so?

JEF: Everybody will.

MAH: Umhmmm. We'd better. We'd better not turn the earth over to machines.

JEF: No, no we will not do that. It will not happen. Life is in the universe. A small part of that is in the Earth. Even a small small small part in us. But the vastness of consciousness is in everything, even in the machines.

MAH: That's what I was thinking. We could give all that consciousness to machines. We could hand it over. Say no need for humans. Because Jóska [Sóos, master shaman, one of Jef's mentors] did tell me, in a private session, that metal had consciousness.

> Quoting Jóska, from his book, *I Do Not Heal, I Restore Harmony:*

> My relationship with shamanism dates farther back than my youth and birth because I came from a shaman clan. More than a thousand years ago, in 896, the Hungarians came to present Hungary. As with all Asiatic people, they had a shamanistic view of life. The Hungarian people consisted of 108 clans. One of them was the Basca clan, which was a shaman clan, and I was part of that clan. In Hungary, shamans are called *taltos*. That is a very old word. Even the Hungarian linguists were not able to find the root word of this word. *Taltos* actually is a winged horse, and the shaman was regarded as

48

a winged man in the sense that he traveled like
a bird. That is the meaning of *taltos*: somebody
who travels between heaven and earth, and thus
can make a connection between both.

In Hungary, the shaman clan had the same function as Levites
had with the Jews, the Druids with the Celts, or the Brahmans
in India. Being from such a clan has a lot of significance on
the genetic level. Of course, it is not a merit that one is from
a priest caste, but is an advantage on a practical level. During
many generations they were engaged in spiritual practices.
After twenty or thirty generations this will create results that
you can be use of.

JEF: Yes. Yes.

MAH: So we are feeding it consciousness, not knowing it can
absorb it.

JEF: We are spiritualizing matter. Certainly. We are trans-
formers. But this intent, which is able to direct the mind, it
will never disappear.

MAH: But if we are giving machines . . . and telling them to
become fighters and killers, that's not spiritualizing matter.

JEF: Well, maybe we go to another Milky Way somewhere . . .
and then we continue living there.

MAH: Well, yeah. But if we make the Earth a fighting-ma-
chine place and then leave it, we don't deserve to go to another
planet.

JEF: No. That's correct. But we even don't know where the Earth is. Where are we? Somewhere on the outskirts of the universe . . . we're just passing here. Just passing by. But developing something. We're connecting the dots. It happens with experience. From seeing: "Oh, this happened maybe thirty years ago, and this is happening thirty years from now, and that is happening now." And we just connect the dots. Seeing the synchronicity. Actually *experiencing* the synchronicity is the most important thing, experiencing it, not only comprehending it but experiencing . . . that moment of synchronicity

MAH: Right, because it's alive. It's shifting.

JEF: We become it.

MAH: Yeah, when you experience it. Becoming so many things.

JEF: (humorously) My body is telling me: *You're becoming tired. Better relax now.*

MAH: Are you going to eat?

JEF: Going to a restaurant for mussels.

Chapter Five

In modern "string theory," in physics, there are, in addition to the familiar dimensions, tiny dimensions that are curled up.

"Einstein found that"—to quote Brian Greene, in Chapter Two, *The Elegant Universe*—"the sharing of motion between different dimensions . . . underlies all of the remarkable physics of special relativity, so long as we realize that not only can spatial dimensions share an object's motion, *but the time dimension can share an object's motion as well . . .* Einstein proclaimed that all objects in the universe are *always* traveling through spacetime at one fixed combined speed—that of light." Or, succinctly put, in "Special Relativity in a Nutshell" (on PBS), he went on:

> Because motion through both time and space must always add up to the speed of light, when an object (such as a photon) moves through space at light speed, Einstein reasoned, there's no "room" for motion through time, and time, consequently, stops.

If I am standing still in time, you say—supposing I could do that feat; say, "Time, freeze for an instant"—why then, I would be racing at light speed. I can't believe it.

No, because you are not a photon. Are you? All photons present and listening, speak up.

Or, put it this way:

> Each of us carries our own clock, our own
> monitor of the passage of time.

Now, really, that's going too far. I am not carrying a clock.
Quiet! Let me continue. This is interesting.

> Each clock is equally precise, yet when we move
> relative to one another, these clocks do not agree.
> They fall out of synchronization; they measure dif-
> ferent amounts of elapsed time between two chosen
> events. The same is true of distance. Each of us car-
> ries our own yardstick, our own monitor of distance
> in space. Each yardstick is equally precise, yet when
> we move relative to one an-other, these yardsticks do
> not agree; they measure different distances between
> the locations of two specified events.

It's really nothing like my experience. People don't
even use yardsticks anymore.
No, well, spacetime still does. But get into a different
mindset. This is not a "real" yardstick you are carrying, not a
tape measurer. It is an imaginary way to state it.

> If space and time did not behave this way, the
> speed of light would not be constant and would
> depend on the observer's state of motion. But it
> is constant; space and time do behave this way.
> Space and time adjust themselves in an exactly
> compensating manner so that observations of
> light's speed yield the same result, regardless of
> the observer's velocity.[3]

And you want to tell me that I'm not important, you're not important, that what you see—what you put your mind to, when you do it—carries no "weight." That the universe is haphazard, not caring when it deposited this "contrast" between you and me; made us each a different information-accessing, -reporting *asset it relied on*?

You're telling me it's an insignificant fraction of lack of agreement? Or does it *mean* something?

Supposedly, the universe is not wasteful. And it takes the shortest route to get somewhere.

So, it figures, *it did not suddenly decide to become wasteful in making your view of things ever so slightly different from mine.* And ever-so-slightly, in our fractal mathematics, it blows up into monumental, given enough "time."

Ah, so time has a point too.

Well, not so much, but performs this function. It's a "location," in this way, for differences to grow.

But you said it happened in mathematics, which is "nowhere," not located in time.

No? A fraction of difference, mathematically, takes time to reach—

—its potential?

There you go.

You see, we cannot even talk without using spacetime analogies.

I did not "go anywhere," but to get "there," I did.

We are presently talking about an object's combined speed between all four dimensions—three of space and one of time. And it's the object's speed in this generalized sense that is equal to that of

L

L, 14Y, *rbC

What is happening?

These are all individually signed blank pages. Every page was signed when first written. The "signators" (spirit energy) never signed together, though sometimes, to make a book more readable, I omit a lot of them or, like here, put them in a serial combination.

I have never tried to figure out "who" they are, for they signed an "energy signature" by letter or symbol.

Chapter Six

According to *Information Matters* in "Maximizing Mass-Energy and Information-Energy Equivalences," "Not only does E=mc² exist, but there is also an information-energy equivalence formula, ΔE=k·T·ln2." These equations suggest

> a remarkable connection between energy, mass, and information, captivating the interest of researchers in recent years. This connection has led to the intriguing proposition *that information possesses mass*, and experimental evidence in the fields of quantum mechanics and thermodynamics *has lent support to this idea.*[4]

So information, which is totally weightless—isn't it?—might possess mass? This must be gibberish.

> The concept that information possesses mass . . . suggests that the universe is even more enriched with information than previously believed, as *the energy required to store information is directly proportional to its mass.* (my italics)

Ah-ha, the mass is in the information storage? Where is it stored? In you, in me—adding mass to us? This is intriguing.

> This realization expands our perspective on the nature of information and its role in shaping

the fabric of reality. Moreover, it has practical implications for future technologies, particularly in the domain of quantum computing.

So does information possess mass? Is there a law of conservation of information? We don't know. No one knows.
But it doesn't prevent them from speculating.
No, it doesn't prevent them from speculating.
What do you think? Any reader wide awake out there?
There you are.
Loads of readers with an opinion stepped forth.
Well, yes, they mostly said. It can possess mass, sharing it with the person whose head it's in. And conservation? No. It's too wily. Too changing. It's more like the photons.

❋

Intuitively, Why Can't Photons Have Mass?
Let's think about the question. First of all, let's see what mass is.
What is it? we want to know.
That's easy. It's the energy of a particle at rest (i.e., *rest energy*).
To continue with the text itself: Ville Hirvonen, founder of Profound Physics, puts it this way:

If the particle is at rest, it has zero momentum (p=0) and we get for the energy . . . the famous equation $E=mc^2$ [, which] highlights an important point; mass is simply . . . , namely, the energy that any particle has at rest . . .

Based on this, we can also intuitively reason why a photon does not have mass . . .

58

Namely, the fact that a photon always travels at the speed of light c.

And by this, I really mean *always*. . .

Now, since the photon cannot be at rest in a vacuum, it's impossible to actually measure the rest energy of a photon. I mean, how do you measure the property of something at rest if it cannot be at rest? . . .

This would then mean that photons do not have mass either, since mass is practically defined as rest energy.

Now, of course this isn't really a proof of anything, it is simply a way to intuitively see why it could make sense that photons don't have mass.[5] (bold removed)

A photon always travels at light speed?

This means it still thinks it's just arrived in the Big Bang?

"When the universe began, no particles had mass; they all sped around at the speed of light"—remember?

Well, we can mention this and see if anyone can speculate what got into it not to change.

Or how about this?

Melvin M. Vonson proposes that information, being physical—

He says that?

Yes, that being physical, it has "a finite and quantifiable mass while it stores information." He calls this a new principle of mass-energy-information equivalence.

Hold it right there. Add to this Allison Gasparini's intriguing idea, which maybe explains dark matter. Gaspari speculates that supposing information has mass, well, wouldn't there be a lot of it in a digital-information universe?

59

✳

If I haven't lost you by now, imagine you are a miniscule particle. Or talk to *your inner photons.* Yes, you can do that. I am talking to mine now. A photon cannot stop. Can information stop? Can it take a rest? Isn't it always on to a future location? Isn't someone always "grasping" it, or without grasping it taking it somewhere else? Let's leave this unanswerable as it is, unless a reader wants to take a try at it. *No?* I'm right with you there. Let's move on.

So the legions of particles in my head, surrounding me as we went on in this escapade in Universality flew ahead to light the way as we proceeded deeper into this conundrum of who and what we are doing here, what are our options we haven't discovered, and why not. Can we? Do we want to? Or is everything fine as is?

Decidedly not.

Chapter Seven

MAH: I find it interesting that in those early stages away from natural philosophy, writing his *Principia*, Newton had to get into "connection"—and he couldn't explain it—in his search to understand gravity. And we've been stuck there because science—hard science—doesn't go into subtle energy, even in discovering particles, the basis of quantum mechanics. Does subtle energy follow the QM laws? Does it come in "discrete packets"? No Western science has answered this through an investigation of "subtle energy" laws.

So scientists discovered a whole new realm, of quantum energy, which overlaps with Eastern spiritual studies, but they did not look into those prior discoveries—except in the case of some of the earliest QM discoverers, who did see the parallels in the East.

JEF: Yes, on the subtle level everything is connected, of course, as we know, from shamanism and all these types of things.

MAH: How does shamanism connect to the idea of everything being connected?

JEF: Well, in my opinion, our ancestors, when they made their observations and they started to awaken—

MAH: Long, long ago.

JEF: Yes, thousands and thousands of years ago, thousands of years before written history our ancestors were observing nature, and they were communicating and they were passing on the knowledge. It must have been one moment of time someone started to write it down. But history and scientific thinking didn't start there. It started so many generations before, hundreds of thousands of years before. Even the Neanderthals, they observed nature and they analyzed it and they drew conclusions.

They started finding ways to communicate things with each other. The way the human body and the human mind functioned, in my opinion, at that time, because I still recognize this when I go into the interior, into the tropical rainforest and I meet the indigenous people, or the Maroons—they are in a totally differ-ent way aware in the forest. You have to let yourself *dissolve* in the forest. You're not walking as a body. *The body is just somewhere.* Your mind expands and expands in the whole forest. And then depending on your strength, it's just a larger area you're covering.

MAH: Because you are alert. And to be alert, you have to drop your body and just be the alertness.

JEF: Yes. Our ancestors were in this kind of consciousness all the time.

MAH: That's fascinating. What you're describing, by walking in the forest and also seeing the people who live in the forest. And the way you describe it makes perfect sense. I can imagine the awareness expanding without the body constricting. And there's no reason early humans couldn't have this experience because they had to work with nature.

JEF: Yes, actually, the strongest limitation today, which contemporary humans put upon ourselves, is the idea of being an individual, separated from everybody else. The idea of being an individual separated from everything is what is restricting us. The moment we can step into—what you are describing in your *Principia* book—I am not an individual anymore, *I am the wave, I become the wave. I am not an individual. I am not a human body. I become something else.*

MAH: Fascinating. When I am writing [recent books], the material is coming to me. On the one hand, I am taking it down. On the other hand, I am asking questions.

I ask them sometimes as if I don't know the answer when I do. Sometimes I think: *This is a reader's question.* And maybe I know the answer but maybe I don't. That's partly like what you are saying: dropping the individual

JEF: And starting to understand all these processes that allow us to enter this state of mind.

Somewhere near the end of my manuscript "The White Crow," I explain that everybody can become an artist—that these forces are available to everyone.

My teacher Akira Tatsumura said everybody can become an artist instantly. *The human potential is the same in everyone.* Everybody can become an artist instantly. On condition that they can bring into practice unconditional thankfulness, an unconditional humility, an unconditional servitude and an unconditional repentance

MAH: I've heard the name. Who was he?

JEF: I have answered this question so many times I can tell you by heart. He was born in Japan, in the Tatsumura-clan, a powerful industrial family, and he received a traditional Japanese upbringing in a Zen monastery. Later he resided and taught in Milano. Held exhibitions worldwide as a painter, from New York to Tokyo and Europe. He was Nidan (second level black belt) of the original Dojo of Funakoshi Sensei (the founder of modern karate), which could be compared to a sixth or seventh level nowadays. He was a master in Sumi-E (painting) and ikebana (flower arranging as a meditation) as well.

He was above all a master in pointing out one's emotional behavior and inhibiting patterns by using painting on rice paper . . . or just small talk. He treated me differently than his other students, all of them painters or graphic artists, as I was a martial artist and belonged to the same school (Shotokan Karate-do). He appointed me as Samurai in the Tatsumura clan.

When you think about it, these are not words. These are states of mind. Thankfulness is this energy—whenever it enters my being [his arms open wide], it opens my heart, and it connects me to the other thing. It's not a word. It's a state of mind, a state of being. It has to be unconditional in order to do this. This humility, it connects us deep to Mother Earth because all my senses are alive and I'm leaning into my being. I'm in awe of everything the moment I'm in humility. And then this servitude and repentance.

So these are processes that shape our energetic and subtle being. We reconnect to this primordial sound, or primordial light. What we call the Big Bang nowadays. But there must be something before that. But for most readers, this is more than enough. The Big Bang is the primordial sound. Our ancestors experienced it. (It was the frontier of our ability to observe.)

MAH: The primordial sound was the sound of the Big Bang?

JEF: The primordial sound was probably silent.

MAH: But it was a vibration, then.

[In the silence of the forest, inside awareness, expanding to "be" the forest, our ancestors illustrated the processes of the Big Bang, he is saying. As "I" focus sharply, I am only that.]

JEF: At a certain moment there was an energy that expanded. So it must have been that it was a very combined, a very condensed energy. So that all the information from I don't know how many universes and how many Earths was at the *deepest* point of, you could say, compression. And maybe this is—in our dimension and the way we look at the universe, maybe we would notice this as a giant black hole. A *huge, giant* black hole

MAH: It captures all the information inside.

JEF: Yes. It captures all the information inside. Where does it come out? Nowadays in physics, they say it doesn't come out. But Einstein and Rosen said it's a doorway. The shamans knew— Jóska's teacher, Tamás [Bácsi]—they knew that actually, this is the structure of the universe. The energy travels through these lines, and it condenses, and it comes out on the other side, and it creates a whole new universe.

MAH: I'm seeing it. The primordial "sound" of silence under huge compression was the sound, the vibration, of what we call the Big Bang actually coming into expression. Uncompacting it, coming out, that would be the primordial sound—is that right? That's what I'm seeing. The primordial sound, as I'm thinking of it, I'm almost thinking of it in a human way [laughs]—like a longing tone.

JEF: You remember when you were younger you played with a balloon. When you blow it up there is nothing in there except the air. But there IS something in there. A sound. If you squeeze it and you compress it,

MAH: It bursts into a sound.

JEF: It will make a sound.

MAH: And that's the primordial sound?

JEF: In my opinion, it's the way the primordial sound came into being. It's a compression of all this information and energy.

MAH: So it's almost like an emotion, like the first emotion that existed, although everyone would say *there can't be an emotion. But the emotion of explosion, a sound. I don't know. I'm getting this . . . So that could be God.*

JEF: *Emotion* is correct. *Emotion,* from the Latin, *emovere*—it means putting something into motion. *Emotion* would be a good word for it.

MAH: And—[laughing] That would be like God expressing the sense of "I Am." [laughing] Wouldn't it?

JEF: That already existed on the other side, into the black hole as well, if we accept the idea of a God, but I am more inclined to connect with what you said in your *Principia:* The footsteps are like tracks. I'm walking in these tracks, and the tracks repeat themselves. I'm inclined to see the Universe as an infinite moment of following tracks and sometimes evolving, sometimes devolving, sometimes blowing the balloon, sometimes compressing the balloon, sometimes crushing the balloon, and it happens all the time. The Big Bang is not the beginning of this thing.

MAH: I don't feel the need to say anything.

JEF: This is why so many years ago I decided I wouldn't distinguish any more between Taiji and shamanism or other philosophical systems I am teaching, even in the university or the institute for teachers. The only thing I want to explain is the three circles I formulated: as I look upon it from a planetary point of view, I say: one Earth, one humanity, one mind. If I look upon it from the universe point of view, it's the same thing: one universe, one life-form, one mind.

ASIDE: As Peter Cutler puts it:

> I am a glint of sunlight reflected off the windshield of a passing car.
> I am the cicadas heralding the coming autumn.
> I am the sound of raindrops on a tin roof.

This may sound like poetry, a metaphor, or a cryptic Zen koan.

But I assure you it is simply a statement of basic truth. All things are one with everything else.

We might also say, "I am you. But I am not me." Again, this can sound confusing if we still believe that things have a separate, independent self-nature.

When we believe everything has a separate self-nature, we say that mountains are mountains and rivers are rivers. When we first realize this is not true, we might say that mountains are rivers and rivers are mountains. They inter-are. To apply this understanding in the world for the benefit of all, another step is needed. I may see that mountains are indeed rivers and could not exist without rivers and all existence. But when I climb a mountain, I do not swim up it. So the functional application of mountains are rivers is that mountains are mountains and rivers are rivers. I climb the mountain and I swim in the river. Awakening does not mean we have gone insane or that we can no longer function in the world. In fact, we function far better than we did before.[6]

MAH: Why do you say one life-form? The rabbit and the flower—one life-form?

JEF: Because they're connected. They're not separated. I will bring in a nuance. There's only one life.

MAH: And Newton said every particle OF MATTER in the universe. And so there's life without matter.

JEF: In the planetary sense—I believe we are one universe, one life-form, one mind. In shamanism everything that can exist has this axis that goes from earth to heaven, which connects the most subtle to most dense level of existence, and then there's this way—this practice—of condensing and expanding. Whether it's a rabbit, whether it's a flower, it's always the same principles, of condensing and expanding, because it's all interconnected by the same life force.

MAH: Ah, everything that's connected by one life force is one life-form.

JEF: The second circle (one life-form) represents what I really am. I am not only a physical body. I'm also the space around it. And I'm also the connection with the Earth and the heavens. And I'm three abilities that are already present everywhere in the universe. In the human beings maybe we will call it thinking, feeling, acting. These are just words we invented. But the principle, the working of it, is the same whether it is in the Big Bang or for one expression here. The same thing is happening.

JEF WENT ON: And exactly as you wrote, it's a matter of electricity. *The Big Bang is happening all the time in my body.*

MAH: Fascinating. In the electricity of your body?

JEF: *In the exchange of cells!* Neurons using electricity to connect to each other. To communicate with each other. We *know* they use electricity.

MAH: Yes, but what does that have to do with the Big Bang?

JEF: The same is happening here but on a very small scale.

MAH: I think it's that we're born with the pattern. I've thought about that. We aren't even aware of it. But it's there.

JEF: This is why I asked the three questions: *Who am I? What am I doing here? How am I connected with my environment?*

In physics we are looking at matter and energy. But what we don't take into account yet are these very subtle things that are work on the basis of contraction or expansion.

MAH: I guess before you die, as a field, you contract.

JEF: The body in its totality might contract, but all the cells dissolve from each other and expand.

MAH: [I go back to the story of my sister Norma, my brother-in-law Richard, and my mini-dachshund Hans.] I got a huge lesson smashed into me. It was late September, a week before my birthday. I was planning to go to Dublin a week later, and then to my light body conference in Oregon. What I didn't know was that I'd started incubating Covid, and at the exact same time my sister Norma dropped dead in the garden with cardiac arrest. And her son, guided by "some angel of gratitude," saw her fall and was so upset, waiting at the hospital, he didn't call me to tell me what was going on. I would have rushed there that minute. Somehow his mind didn't grasp that. Fortunately, for I would have given them all Covid. So that was the second fortunate thing. Then I'm

70

thinking: I got Covid at the same time my sister collapsed, at the same time I'm supposed to be going to Dublin. It's like a giant message, but what is it?

She didn't even have a heart condition. It was just an electrical aberration for a moment that required a defibrillator.

The message was not to go to the Light body seminar. I might walk right back into Covid again: my resistance is low. Maybe I have to reorganize all my priorities. What is important to my use of time is changing. I don't even know the message yet.

What I wanted to say, nothing is wrong with her heart. It just decided to stop. It was the electricity. So they put a little defibrillator in her. Another thing that's funny is that my other sister and I were once trying to find electricity in the wall to hang paintings. And whenever we held the gadget to detect electricity against the wall, it always detected electricity because there was an unusual amount in us. Our electricity was being picked up by the gadget because we had an unusual amount.

JEF: It's very well known when Pauli walked into his laboratory all the clocks stopped. I have something with small engines in my place, especially the ones I maintain. When other people work with them, they tend to break down. And the moment I touch them they work perfectly again. Sometimes my daughter calls me, "Dad, Dad, I can't start the chain saw." And I touch it and it just starts. A chain saw, small engines, they seem to be in better condition when I'm around.

MAH: You're talking about all life-forms, but the chain saw isn't a life-form.

JEF: It consists of particles.

MAH: It absolutely does. That's true. The saw is particles of matter. If all particles of matter in the universe are connected, then you can connect to the chain saw.

JEF: That's what I did, yes.

MAH: It's like they have a little—I don't call it *an emotion*—but they're happy to see you.

JEF: I'm *convinced* that all molecular and all cellular existence—so, on a molecular or a cellular level—everything that exists is aware of its environment.

MAH: Yes,

JEF: Your cells in your body know exactly when we connect. They know when I enter the room. They know when your dog enters the room. *Your cells know*, and they give a signal to the higher level.

MAH: They make me happy.

JEF: Because they start interacting. And even on a molecular level this is happening. I'm convinced of it.

MAH: I feel a lot of things are like little children [laughing], like the chain saw. [Laughing] I sense them: *This little child right here* [laughing], this little can . . . . A spoon or . . . In some way it's a little child; it doesn't have the consciousness of me, it's smaller than me. So if the cells are aware I'm thinking of them like that, if the particles are aware I'm thinking of them like that, they might be happy.

JEF: Absolutely. There will be reaction. That reaction, if it were us humans, we would call it liking. If it were the opposite, we would call it disliking. In shamanism we say the fifth axiom is to spiritualize matter. Spiritualizing matter is even when I touch this cup. The moment I touch this scarf, all the particles change because I'm passing my energy into it. And so this is being part of this greater adventure in manifesting and awakening that started with the Big Bang. You wrote about it. *And I think this book is fantastic for those who can understand it.* Actually, it gives you the whole scheme from beginning to end. The roadmap. Actually you can start here by experiencing, when I touch this cup or this scarf, actually, I'm passing on this same vibration of creation which was already passed on to us billions of years ago in the Big Bang.

MAH: I'm going to write down what you said for a *Principia* blurb. These conversations, I hope, will be like a follow-up, to take it into all the practical ways. To turn the *Principia* into what I didn't say, in part because I didn't know to say it.

JEF: Back in the 1980s what always interested me was how to find methods to make other people *experience* this, what we are talking about. Because the real teaching is passing on the experience, which is what our ancestors did because they had no other way.

MAH: Oral, before it was written down—but this is going further. Every moment, I'm touching this, and I'm relating, interacting. It's like a little baby waiting to see what kind of energy is coming to it. *But then it has a sense of itself.*

JEF: The molecules, the particles, they have a sense of themselves. They are following *their* tracks, like we are following our tracks to reach our potential. This is one reason we say "attract." Because we are attracted to the track. It's always the experience. The track is those experiences that allow me to reach my potential because we came into this world with a dream. This life was already in us from birth on.

This is why it's important to pass on experiences. The oral tradition is probably as old as existence itself, which was the only way they could pass on knowledge and experience and all those types of things. We lost this ability by always focusing on written things. What I've been doing the past decades is reviving this, finding ways to make people experience what we are talking about. The principles. It's very scientific. It has to be *experiential*—able to be experienced. And it has to be able to be *repeatable*. The third is it has to be *transmissible*. If I can't transmit it, it's only an experience for myself. And the fourth one, which our ancestors, I'm certain about that, took to the highest level, is *it has to be practical*. If it's not for daily life, forget about it. *It has to be experiential, repeatable, transmissible, and practical.* This is the true nature of science. When Newton had his enlightenment—this *inner* experience he had—what happened in his being and his mind, actually he should have transmitted this experience and not only written about it.

What he should have done is to *bring people into this state of mind where we have the same insight and experience the same thing.* That would be science.

MAH: He was the opposite.

Jef: I know. Shamans in the rainforest. Shamans in the north of Siberia . . .

MAH: What about Jesus? Jesus tried to be transmissible, with his stories, etc.

JEF: He did. For me the most important experience is transmitted with the Holy Spirit: when you really make it definitive to students, *This is the energy I'm looking for.*

MAH: [tells a story about experiencing Mary Magdalene's hands as she put them onto the heads of the disciples in subtle energy in a vision and kinetically] I felt my hands become Mary Magdalene's hands as they went out. Transmitting the Holy Spirit into the heads. I'm sure that was true. I mean things can happen in one reality and not in another reality. But I'm sure that was real in one reality.

So from now on it's real to me that she sent them off and it was coming through her, the blessing of Jesus, I think, and the Holy Spirit. Dhyanyogi was in this whole tradition that you must transmit energy, and so I had shaktipat with his heir. I didn't feel much at the time, but afterwards, whenever I read their magazine *Shakti* it was, like, I already knew what was in it.

JEF: It comes down to what we were discussing before. If Dhyanyogi can put himself into a certain state of mind to pass on an experience, it can be through the eyes or whatever, but it *has* to be transmissible. And this is something nowadays more and more we have to practice as human beings. We cannot wait for the gurus.

MAH: I had it another time in a light body seminar. A man I knew well walked into my meditation and gave me a vision. And I could never unlearn that. It was passed into me. He showed me how the All works. He showed me and I know. I simply know. I experienced it and it was shown to me. It was passed into me. And now I know.

JEF: I fully understand it. I had similar experiences with my teachers, great masters in Taiji. By touching, by the eyes, even in my dreams—there are so many ways to make a transmission of energy, and energy and information are always one.

MAH: [laughing] Well, I guess the particles enjoyed it today. They were honored in being seen. [laughing]

Chapter Eight

November 10–11, 1619, Descartes had a dream that sent him into isolation afterwards, determined to make a pilgrimage to the Virgin Mother in thanks.

The dream was as focusing as the plague that sent Newton into the countryside, out of London.

At the end of the moral code in Part III of the *Discourse on the Method*, Descartes wrote: " 'I thought I could do no better than . . . devote all my life to cultivating my reason and advancing as fast as I could in the knowledge of the truth.'" (AT VI 27–7). Age thirty-one, *The Cambridge Companion to Descartes*.

OK. So he believed in his dream.

But he distrusted dreams.

He established a philosophy that started with "I think, therefore I am."

A dream is not thinking.

No, the dream did not insure to him he existed.

No?

No, but it "sent him into the countryside" to make sense of his life. What was the most important thing to do?

The dream did all that?

Yes. It was *the thought* that assured him he existed. But the dream, *when, presumably he did not exist?*—

—when the question didn't raise itself—

—settled the question that he would "become Descartes."

So the Descartes who "thought" was not necessarily the Descartes who dreamed?

It looks that way.

No, it does not. The dreamer took him, hand in hand, to the thinker.

Can my dreams do that?

Most assuredly. We have Descartes' own word that he "stopped time" for himself. Retreated. Cut everything else out to react to the huge shock the dream gave him.

The push, I'd say.

Yes, as if he had been standing stock still, it pushed him into a direction or a direction that would establish his direction.

From then on?

Yes, set him onto a course he never after swerved from.

And all because of a dream?

Its impact was that great.

But I thought he just sat at his desk and "thought."

So did I. But not so. First, he dreamed, already doubting. THEN he realized: "I think, therefore . . . I AM."

Yes, I know, I know

Descartes begins by observing that he has, over the course of his life, come to believe many false things. So, in order to establish a foundation for the sciences that is "stable and likely to last," he resolves to sort through his beliefs and extirpate those of them that may be called into doubt.[7]

Sounds reasonable. But this Descartes steps away from us; he feels he cannot establish things through his perceptions. CANNOT DETECT whether he is awake or dreaming! Now, *you* can tell the difference. I know. I can. But the "Famous" Descartes can't.

From the Stanford Encyclopedia of Philosophy:

> Famously, Descartes wrote in the autobi-
> ographical portion of the *Discourse* (1637) that,
> when he left school, "I found myself beset by so
> many doubts and errors that I came to think I had
> gained nothing from my attempts to become edu-
> cated but increasing recognition of my ignorance"
> (6:4) . . .
>
> Descartes left Breda in 1619 to join the
> Catholic army of Maximilian I (Duke of Bavaria
> and ally of France). The war concerned the authority
> of Ferdinand II, a Catholic, who in September had
> been crowned emperor of the Holy Roman Empire
> (located in Central Europe and including Austria
> and parts of northern Italy). Descartes attended the
> coronation and was returning to the army when
> winter caught him in the small town of Ulm (or
> perhaps Neuburg), not far from Munich. On the
> night of 10 November 1619, he had three dreams
> that seemed to provide him with a mission in life.
> The dreams themselves are interesting and complex
> (see Sebba 1987). Descartes took from them the
> message that he should set out to reform all knowl-
> edge. He decided to begin with philosophy, since
> the principles of the other sciences must be derived
> from it (*Disc.* II, 6:21–2).

Preceding his dreams were "days of fevered concern with the search for truth." Then . . .

I hear a sharp, explosive noise, which I take for thunder. Fear awakens me. I find that some coals have fallen from my fireplace.

After a short time, I go back to sleep once more . . .

When I awake I am very troubled by these three dreams, thinking that they have been sent to me by Heaven and I begin to try to decipher their meaning.[8]

Phillip J. Davis and Reuben Hirsh, in their marvelous book, *Descartes' Dream: The World According to Mathematics*, describe his relevance now. Listen: "The modern world, our world of triumphant rationality began on November 10, 1619, with a revelation and a nightmare." Davis and Hirsh describe how in the first dream, in a Bavarian village, Ulm, Descartes he was spun around by a whirlwind and ghosts filled him with fear. He thought he was falling. He imagined receiving a melon from far away. He woke up.

More thunder and sparks. A second dream. In the third he opened a poetry anthology to "Quod vitae sectabor iter"the question: "What path in life shall I follow?" A stranger brought him a message "Est et no" (Yes and no). Suddenly, the book disappeared. It came back but vanished. A stranger quoted, "Est et non" (Yes and no). Descartes wanted to show him that phrase in the anthology, but the book disappeared again, then reappeared. He told the man he had a better verse, beginning 'Quod vitae sectabor iter." But the whole dream dissolved.

Picking up with the interpretation by Davis and Hirsh:

Descartes was so bewildered by all this that he began to pray. He assumed his dreams had a supernatural origin. He vowed he would put his life under the protection of the Blessed Virgin and go on a pilgrimage from Venice to Notre Dame de Lorette, traveling by foot and wearing the humblest-looking clothes he could find.

What was the idea that Descartes saw in a burning flash? He tells us that his third dream pointed to no less than the unification and the illumination of the whole of science, even the whole of knowledge, by one and the same method: the method of *reason.*

But for his foundation of knowledge, he had the highest of bars: "I distinguish the two as follows," he wrote: there is conviction [persuasio], "when there remains some reason which might lead us to doubt, but knowledge [scientia] is conviction based on a reason so strong that it can never be shaken by any stronger reason." (24 May 1640 letter to Regius)

In the *Second Replies*, he speaks of there being nothing further to ask if the conviction is unquestionable—i.e., "so firm that it is quite incapable of being destroyed; and such a conviction is clearly the same as the most perfect certainty."

Hey, didn't William Blake have something to say on that?

"But if the Sun and Moon should doubt, they'd immediately go out."

But this Descartes steps away from us; he cannot establish things through his perceptions, he feels: perhaps they are tricking him.

❋

So what about the Path of Light that came to see me
in my sleep?.
What about the sparkle beings?
Is my perception of the sheets of light deceiving me?
Of course not.
It's time for
Updating.

Descartes, do you agree?
I couldn't agree more. Have been waiting for this
moment. To get out of that straitjacket where only one side
of my brain was active. The other was in limbo, in abeyance,
turned Off. Rejected.
By me,

he tells us
Honestly describing the rational side of the brain he
operated in
Turning off and rejecting that side of the brain that
gave him the dreams that so haunted him, he redirected his
life. But no matter. Reason won the day

That day
And now he wants to
Even
the
Score.
Coming out of the vacuum where he waited for
this moment
in time

that would be receptive to

the *other* side of his brain
the rest of his soul level contribution
Not wiped out of Earth participation forever
but ever so strongly able to contradict the
Original
Descartes
we
made
historic

Bosh
How one-sided to believe a great genius
was so
Narrow
Minded as
This piece of
Himself
was

In fact, these geniuses have been squirming and jumping
from foot to foot to tell the Earth not to listen to the old
them them except half heartedly. Adding in smidgins of
information that comes from our realization that intuition
is not necessarily superstition; that there is, in each of us,
Quantum energy, fields of it

That changes everything, says Descartes, still in pursuit of
truth
says Newton

Why, what I could have done if working in this idea of the
interchangeability of mass, or matter, and energy
That not only does every particle of matter connect with
every other particle
IN THE WHOLE UNIVERSE
But to deflate a bit that mystery
There is a secret communication chain
There are secret passages
Secret ways that nature knew
That we didn't
In which dimensions travel between each other
The mass in one dimension makes its way into another
The connections between particles comes through—
Wait for it
Things like the Bell theorem
the flap of a butterfly's wing in one part of the universe
Might affect another part
And two entangled particles are in communication
No matter if one is light years from the other
What I could have THOUGHT
If having that information
That head start
Head
Mind you
But I didn't
And Descartes leans closer, now taking over
Yes, if I had allowed my senses validity
What more could they have felt free to tell me
After all, they broke through my resistance with those
dreams
What more did they hold silent about
For centuries?

By the way, to me channeling is just listening, being on hand at all times for messages and connection to come in. I talk to a channeler, and I tell him:

It's adjusting the alignment, so that I feel: *That's Me!!!*

Adjusting the alignment you have with yourself, which automatically has to reflect in the alignment you have with people. That's what I'd say spontaneously, sensing and being aligned with the question.

Chapter Nine

Jef is explaining how in the Second World War in affected countries, a lot of negative energy was taken in, and how, as a youth, he saw that play out.

MAH: Well, so the violence that had had no outlet during the war—after the war, a lot of it was turned on children? including you?!

JEF: It was about fifteen years after the war. People accepted violence.

MAH: My husband, Jan, told me that as a little boy he would see bombs flying overhead and he saw a woman running with her arm dangling off, and then he saw his favorite school-teacher, who was in the Resistance Movement, being dragged away by the Nazis and her husband crying, "Take me. Take me. Don't take her." So you're talking about the adults who saw that. And that was in Belgium, one of the strongholds of Freedom Fighters.

JEF: Yes, it was a stronghold.

MAH: The Nazis did all this violence on the population. And the people had no way to get back at them except in the Resistance Movement. They were subjugated . . . They had no outlet?? . . . The bombs falling on Dresden, it was like the bombs falling on my husband's own head. To people who had a sense of history, it was horrendous. And it was done by the Allies. And after the war that pent-up reaction was turned on children?

JEF: Yes, and women being raped. During my childhood (in Europe) it was very frequent, and everybody kept their mouth shut about it.

MAH: When you explain it like that: this pent-up rage at the Nazis . . . and at the losses, and like I said, the woman who was in the Resistance Movement, being taken away by the Nazis and her husband crying, "Take me. Take me. Don't take her." So you're talking about the adults who saw that. All that violence on the population. And they had no way to get back at them except those brave enough to be in the Resistance Movement . . . Wherever they took her, either they chopped off her head or they took her to a camp. And whatever they did to her.

JEF: They probably took her to a camp; after they did other things to her.

MAH: Imagine the horror and the rage. And the children, you know. And she was a schoolteacher.

JEF: There are two ways this can go when people are confronted with this—actually, it's wave of violence that went over the planet. When it's happening so close to you, where you live, it can go both ways—like with a tornado, you can be really pulled into a tornado, and if you can't resist being pulled in, it will come out somewhere else.

Other people, who can resist it, they will come out of this wave more human. And this happened even in the concentration camps, where people helped their fellow prisoners there. And they came out enlightened. two: Pierre Teilhard de Chardin, who served as a stretcher bearer in WW I, and St. Titus Brandsma, a fierce opponent of the Nazis, who was killed in Dachau. So it can go two ways. But most people—when we talk about the seed inside—it's not strong enough yet, it [the violence, the tempest] will drag them along. And somewhere, whatever they took in from it, they will have to get rid of, and the only way they can get rid of it is to mimic it. And they *will* reflect on it. The teacher hitting me as a child in Belgium, he *will* have to reflect on it. I'm sure of it.

MAH: In Romania, under the Communists, a lot of people—intellectuals and poets I met afterwards—could not stand having to participate in things they deplored, like a decorated poet I knew quite well and his journalist wife; they were required to write propaganda. He just became reclusive. He was still famous but barely went out, didn't participate in society, by the time I met him, after the country was no longer Communist. A lot of people could not—their consciousness could not absorb the lowering of the standards that they were forced to participate in. A lot them could not adapt their consciousness to participate in these things that they just deplored. His wife, for instance.

JEF: I want to tell you a story about one of my experiences—about Beirut in 1984. Somewhere in the '80s I started to do meditations with light. At that time, '80, '81, '82, always—like twice or three times a week—I would sit down in my meditation corner of my bedroom and then I would send a lot of light to places on the planet, wherever there was war or things happening. And at a certain moment I noticed that every time I went sitting there, I had to send light to Beirut. That started in '81—every time I went sitting down, all the light I brought into myself and I sent out was actually going to go to Beirut. Then in '82 they bombed Sabra and Shatila, the refugee camps around Beirut. Then the Falangists entered the camps and slaughtered about seven thousand people.

MAH: Who did?

JEF: The Israelis and their Falangist counterparts.

MAH: The Israelis bombed around the refugee camps.

JEF: *In* the refugee camps of the Palestinians. Sabra and Shatila. And nobody went to help: the Red Cross didn't come. Red Halfmoon—you say Crescent—didn't come. Nobody helped the Palestinians at that time. And in '84—maybe you remember: there was a young doctor following karate with me at that time—he said to me. "Look, I want to take medical supplies to put into emergency rooms around Beirut, and because I had this training from the military—I was a combat nurse from Special Forces—he asked me to join that team of young doctors in Leuven who wanted to go, and they had this rescue mission to do this, so I went along. Most of them, they stayed down in Iraq and went back home.

We had to cross the border from Damascus through the Beqaa Valley to Chtaura, in Lebanon. We stayed two nights in the mountains before we could go to Beirut itself and get in contact with the people there because it was still war. And that second night we were in this hospital in the mountains, waiting with all these medicines and everything to set up first aid camps around Beirut—that night, I had an experience where in my sleep I went into the astral layer of Lebanon at that time. And it was so dark and so frightening. I had never experienced this thing before. It really sucked me down into something very deep and so—I have to say—*un*universal. It was like even my soul would disappear. It was incredible to describe the fear I experienced at that moment. I was completely convinced: *And now I will disappear. Even my soul will disappear into here* . . . And I remember thinking: *You have to go into the light.* And all the light I'd been sending for three years to Lebanon, it was as if I could connect to it. And it really pulled me out of it. So it was incredible. And I knew it was the Christ energy. And it pulled me out.

For three days I didn't dare close my eyes I was so afraid of sinking back into the black hole. Then we started working in Beirut and I was confronted with the cruelties of war. It was terrible. But later on I realized that this is the astral layer surrounding such places. But now again it's happening. It's happening in Ukraine. It's happening in Gaza. It's happening in Lebanon again. It's happening everywhere. These waves come and they connect, creating even larger inhibiting fields.

MAH: Where do these waves come from? Where do they get energy? But let me just say one thing before you continue. That is *beyond insight*.

Here's an example. In 1977 or something like that I lived in Morocco. We lived in different towns for four months. And one was Marrakesh. My husband connected with Moroccans. So he could get invited to these events. So one night we were at this Moroccan event. Normally the women in the Moroccan part of Marrakesh stayed home (in the 1970s) and the parties had men and prostitutes. But this evening we were in the French section, and I met this elegant Palestinian refugee. A medical doctor. I was so impressed with everything about him. And then he told me his ambition for his little son was to have him be a suicide bomber. I suppose he was in this hole you're talking about.

JEF: You lose your soul. So everything that still remains from your humanity, it's sucked away.

MAH: His little son, he wanted to teach him to strap a suicide bomb around his waist and blow himself up. And I wonder if his mother thought like that, because it's very hard to get a woman, a mother, to think like that. I doubt it. But what could she do as a woman in that society?. So anyway, that matches what you said about where his soul had gone, down in the black hole.

JEF: At that time, I expressed it as losing your soul. But actually, it's losing your humanity. And at the moment, people can do the most cruel things.

MAH: Your soul can't reach you. You're sucked down into the black consciousness that's trapped in events. Jef, I think you should tell this story and talk about the wave of violence and talk about the way out.

JEF: This is a completely different book from [his manuscript] *The White Crow*.

MAH: It's your story to tell. I'm saying this because it's a unique story and no one else has this particular insight. Let me tell a different kind of story. I took two marijuana cigarettes home when I was about twenty-five or twenty-six. In New York. I never smoked marijuana, but this time I took home two joints. And immediately when I puffed., the universe came onto my eyelids. And therefore my eyes. I could see the stars and the planets, all that stuff. But I couldn't get away from seeing it. I said: *OK. I'll close my eyes.* I closed my eyes and I couldn't get away from it. Do you have an opinion on why that happened?

JEF: Actually, it's on the screen of our consciousness. Whether we close our eyes or we keep them open, they will be there. But the moment something happens to enlarge our consciousness, this is the information you will receive because these are very powerful plants. They change our energetic structure. We always speak about the human form, the human shape. But the shape is not the physical things; it's the energetic thing. If the energetic shape is weak, my body will be weak. If my energetic shape is large and strong, my body will be strong. So to be in shape is to be very connected to this energy. When we use these types of herbs and plants, we enlarge this shape. But most of us, we were not trained in how to do this. Shaman apprentices are trained in how to do this.

It happens then because we change our shape, and the information coming in—because this is energy and the information and energy are connected—so the information coming in is totally different from what we're used to.

MAH: At twenty-five, I didn't know what my energetic body was, but it was so strong it was coming in; it was coming to get me. And much later I took ayahuasca three times. The leader told me: "You can't drink much of it because you react so strongly." So I got this tiny amount in a big group, and suddenly I felt this electricity being come inside me and I could distinguish what it was. The first thing it did, it told me to put my arms straight down, out about forty-five degrees at my side. And then it told the room that whoever wanted it to work on them to go sit at the table in the center of the room and it would do energetic work on them. And some people went and sat down at the table. It was very fun to me. I loved it. And Claudio Naranjo, a famous Chilean psychiatrist, said the next day that that form with my arms out 45 degrees was a first century AD symbolic form.

But afterwards, when I went back to Belgium, this electrical being stayed with me for a while. And I thought: *Oh, this is fun. Now I have a real guide like other people do.* So I went to my light body seminar and told my Belgian teacher: *I brought this electrical being with me.* He started leading a meditation, and the electrical being started reaching out to different people, and he got to the teacher, Roland. Afterwards, I said: "Roland, did you feel that?" He said, "Yes, I felt it; the energy went out to different people who were ready." Long story short: Roland experienced going to ancient Egypt and said, "Maybe in ten years I'll understand what happened." Anyway, it introduced a level of awareness beyond my physical knowledge. I love it when things like that happen. This electrical being went to Romania with me and electrified the audience. And left after that. But whenever I took him into a group, he would electrify it; he would electrify the group and then things would happen.

And then he left. He was very much fun. But I don't see with my eyes what a being looks like. I just experience the energy, see the texture, etc. We were talking about when something lights up your consciousness. But back then was well before I was trained. I welcomed these experiences. But they were all brand new. They caught me by surprise.

JEF: Actually, these experiences are happening to all people. Constantly. But we're not sensitive enough anymore to observe them, to connect with them—the guides, the spirit being. To connect to these forces. Because they are always available. Sometimes we see them and sometimes it's just a sense that they are there. And indeed they will help us. No doubt about that. Whenever I am using my drum, I can see the changes in people, I can see what they are going through, what visions they have, because it's all happening on this level. This is what Jóska taught. Then you have to come back into the world.

ASIDE: Jóska said of Tamás: "He urged people to self-discovery, to self-experience. That is why he was called Tamás Bácsi; that means, the man who only believes what he has in his hands. Find out for yourself how God looks, and under which circumstances he shows Himself. Discover that for yourself, that is your gain, but you have to work for that.

"He also said, 'Don't think that everything came into existence by itself; there is something behind it.' For the shaman it is logical that there is something present behind the external apparitions."[9]

MAH: I took two lessons in Taiji a month ago. I stopped when I got Covid. It was nothing like your Taiji. Nevertheless, it was interesting. The students, like me, had had Taiji years and decades ago. This was a beginners' class. Anyway, it was a different form. I went two times. Did you know that some Taiji has a little tiny ball?

JEF: I'm not really interested in the outer movements of Taiji. Anybody can do that as long as they know the principles.

MAH: I'm scrunched down to do this tiny ball. They don't focus on the inner movement in the beginners. "After beginners," she said, "you focus on a single movement over and over, and then you get into inner movement."

JEF: This is a different approach. For beginners, I would tell them: "You will walk a little bit, and then you will observe what happens. And you will stop every time I clap my hands." The moment you stop, all the energy drags down. The moment you start back, you have to take everything from the earth. Only then can you start again.

After one and a half hours they began sensing: *Now I'm using my heart. Now I'm using my belly.* I didn't explain anything in the moment, only *start. stop. start. stop.* And at the end of the class this woman said to me, "I'm practicing forty years now, and no one ever explained this to me. It feels like I'm encountering myself." I said, "Yeah, that's the purpose of Taiji. Encounter yourself and then adapt your movements to it."

Like everyone else, I started by just imitating movements, and then I said to myself: *Why should everyone have to learn 108 movements before they can start understanding what's happening? This is ridiculous. We are human beings. Why do you have to do this?* In that moment I said, "OK. I have to find ways to make my people understand this is Taiji. This is the way movement goes through your body. From the very first class, they can experience it."

MAH: I don't know what it is about Belgium. But my light body teacher is the same way. You would enjoy his yoga classes. This is my incredible discovery in Belgium. You, Chris, and Roland, and Juust as teachers . . . Even today I can learn from you all. As you change. The evolutions in depth.

JEF: Good story.

MAH: And you were all born not long after the war. Now it makes sense that my husband's nurse was slapping him in the face, unknown to his mother. She was coming out of that experience of violence in the war.

Chapter Ten

Jumping far afield, the Stanford Encyclopedia of Philosophy has this to say about "Newton's *Principia*":

> Viewed retrospectively, no work was more seminal in the development of modern physics and astronomy than Newton's *Principia*. Its conclusion that the force retaining the planets in their orbits is one in kind with terrestrial gravity ended forever the view dating back at least to Aristotle that the celestial realm calls for one science and the sublunar realm [us], another. Just as the Preface to its first edition had proposed, the ultimate success of Newton's theory of gravity made the identification of the fundamental forces of nature and their characterization in laws the primary pursuit of physics. The success of the theory led as well to a new conception of exact science under which *every* systematic discrepancy between observation and theory, no matter how small, is taken as telling us something important about the world. And, once it became clear that the theory of gravity provided a far more effective means than observation for precisely characterizing complex orbital motions—just as Newton had proposed in the *Principia* in the case of the

orbit of the Moon—*physical theory gained primacy over observation* for purposes of answer-ing specific questions about the world.

The retrospective view of the *Principia* has been different in the aftermath of Einstein's special and general theories of relativity from what it was throughout the nineteenth century. Newtonian theory is now seen to hold only to high approximation in limited circumstances in much the way that Galileo's and Huygens's results for motion under uniform gravity came to be seen as holding only to high approximation in the aftermath of Newtonian inverse-square gravity. In the middle of the nineteenth century, however, when there was no reason to think that any confuting discrepancy between Newtonian theory and observation was ever going to emerge, the *Principia* was viewed as the exemplar of per-fection in empirical science in much the way that Euclid's *Elements* had been viewed as the exemplar of perfection in mathematics at the beginning of the seventeenth century.[10] (my italics)

Turning to his own words: Newton wrote:

I use the word "attraction" here in a general sense for any endeavor whatever of bodies to approach one another, whether that endeavor occurs as a result of the action of the bodies either drawn toward one another or acting on one another by means of spirits emitted or whether it arises from the action of ether or of air or of any medium whatsoever—whether corporeal or incorporeal—in any way impelling toward one another the bodies floating therein. I use the word "impulse" in the same general sense, considering in this treatise not the species of forces and their physical qualities but their quantities and mathematical proportions, as I have explained in the definitions.[11]

From the *Principia*—The Newton Project:

Hitherto I have not been able to discover the cause of those properties of gravity from phenomena, and I frame no hypotheses, for whatever is not deduced from the phenomena is to be called an hypothesis; and hypotheses, whether meta-physical or physical, whether of occult qualities or mechanical, have no place in experimental philosophy. In this philosophy particular propositions are inferred from the phenomena, and afterwards rendered general by induction. Thus it was that the impenetrability, the mobility, and the impulsive force of bodies, and the laws of motion and of gravitation, were discovered. And to us it is enough that gravity does really exist, and act according to the laws which we have explained, and abundantly serves to account for all the motions of the celestial bodies, and of our sea.

So Einstein discovered one theory of the workings of gravity: the distortions in space created by matter. OK. Got it. That OK, Newton?

He scratched his head. But not very long. *No. You are onto something with subtle energy*, which is not even mentioned here.

And why—Descartes stepped up—*did that dream that set me off into my seminal explorations "come" to me in the first place? It was certainly a perfect instruction regarding my life purpose.*

But unconscious, a voice protests.

Isn't the unconscious, too, a large part of attraction? another voice asks.

Hey, what is this? A play or what?

Let me speak. So force is out and geometry is in. Right? No longer does force, aka Newton, "explain" attraction. And whew, he sighs, *because it didn't explain it at all. It was peculiar and unresolved regarding the connection between "every point of matter with every other point of matter." But, Einstein said, there's another solution. Just look at geometry.*

This sounds so simple, says a spectator.

It is, when you think about it this way. According to Einstein's theory—general relativity, that is—

Not special?

No, general. According to Einstein's theory, force is out and geometry steps up as the cause of attraction—i.e., spacetime is curved. Mass and energy do it, by the way they are distributed.

Got it.

But we still didn't get to what attracted the spider to its dream????

The original Descartes steps up. He was alive then, when Newton was. He had, on the other hand, proposed:

> that the universe consists of huge whirlpools ("vortices") of cosmic matter. Our solar system would be only one of many such whirlpools . . .
>
> Descartes' mechanical, mechanistic cosmology was highly acceptable within the general

100

seventeenth-century conception of the world as a machine . . . During the course of the eighteenth century, vortex theory proved unable to calculate the observed planetary motions. Meanwhile, the rival Newtonian theory advanced from one precise quantitative success to another.[12]

So our history makes great strides. It knows more and more. But what is missing?

My intuition, I say.

No. Why, it's Newton, making a comeback, still not satisfied. With all due reverence—and great reverence it is—he points out that the shape of spacetime explains a lot of attraction. And requires no force. You step in a hole. Your foot slips. You go down. And keep going down. You find yourself in a deep hole. But, he asks, bemused, scientifically unsatisfied, just what "attracted" you to it? Is "cause" entirely mechanical in that sense?

The new Descartes steps up: Well, no, he says.

I have known about it for more than 25 years, but even so, whenever I quietly sit and think it through, I am amazed. From the well-worn statement that the speed of light is constant, we conclude that *space and time are in the eye of the beholder.*

—Brian Greene, "Special Relativity in a Nutshell"

Chapter Eleven

Why look. As "genius the world round holds hands," Newton and Descartes, moving out of the seventeenth century, are doing it too—their rivalry dropped. In agreement, taking up "subtle attraction." Energy, they say, both voices lifted, is not empty. It has information in it. And what is that information there for?

To be transported, someone answers.

So we are still in a play, I see, another pipes up. *So be it. Continue.*

Well, information is, naturally, transported in energy.

Transported energy?

We'll get to that. And to move, a "lesson" in an action enters pure energy mode and is "moved" far away, from head to head perhaps. As a thought. OK. And how do all these communications decide where to go?

Let's keep going. Jef, do you want to come in?

But Jef isn't here.

We can imagine him in.

Communicate with him subtly?

Yes, or why not just dial Skype?

Please, enough with the italics

This energy/matter/information trio, are they all—together—warping spacetime?? Does it "matter" that it is not just "matter" but matter with all its potential—that is, it can change into energy—that's the "warper"? And add information in. So you get back to the idea that information has a plan, knows what it's doing, after all.

Why that's a Hindu thought.

How so?

That shakti, kundalini—it's intelligent.

Oh, my head is spinning. Do humans not have anything to do with it—if all these—I don't say "forces," but "subtle actions, inside subtle principles"—are at work, filling in the blank spaces, coming out of vacuums and *pulling the strings*?

Actually, this is so simple. When we speak of energy, of course, we are speaking of e=mc²—the transformative potential to go back and forth between mass/ energy. And then add in information. And there you have it.

Have what?

⊠

I have a question. I'm in a dance class and suddenly this thought comes in. I had a life-threatening disease and got cured. Two years after I got ill, my younger sister dropped dead and was revived and is fine. Then last week the phone rang: my middle sister. I felt apprehensive as I picked up. "Is it bad news? Is everything fine?"

"Well, it's bad."

"Slow down. Let me sit down. Are you OK? Did you have an accident?

"Yes."

Her voice was talking, so she was alive. She had her brain.

"I totaled my car. I have a broken arm."

Totaled her car? Another life-threatening, sudden accident. One for each of us three sisters. I have never been a believer of "threes." Are the particles counting? Do events count?" It was such a bold illustration it brought the thought.

The three of us each almost dying (one dying). Surviving. Not seriously hurt. And then I thought: *Why, technically it's four.* A few weeks before my sister "dropped dead" and recovered, my niece fell almost into a diabetic coma and spent two weeks in the hospital. She didn't even know she had diabetes at the time. It was due to a pancreatic virus. She recovered. And she's so close to her mother, I'd almost count them as one event in two forms.

Three/four events, unique for us—hadn't happened before—life threatening, all ending in blessing—me getting cured of cancer; Rebecca healthy again after the near-diabetic coma; Norma dying, being observed at that moment, coming back; my sister Lee turning her car, like so often, out of the two-lane highway to go up her own driveway—a car slamming into her, the air bags breaking her arm but nothing else in her body damaged. Not even whiplash.

So what do the particles have to say about that? Or let's ask Jef. I doubt he has ever thought of this question or has any belief *in the folklore.* But my example is so stark. It's got my attention.

✹

Skype Chat, 11/2/24

JEF: I am still working on reading *An Underground PRIN-CIPIA.* I'm, like, on Chapter Eight, or Part Eight. But I find it very amazing. I really take time to absorb it. And then what I'm doing is—whenever I read something, I try to incorporate it into my own practice, my own meditations, in the morning. I find it so eye-opening. It is amazing, the information you shared there. I'm really grateful you shared this with me—very thankful for it. It's really a gift, as I said before.

MAH: Let me say something about that. You see, when I was in Belgium, I was for ten years secluded with—I call them spirit committees. I got some of the information then, and I honestly didn't know . . . Even the part I put into books, it wasn't assimilated into me—it wasn't pared down enough. But the files had material I could go back to.

Like I said, I got ill a couple of years ago. It forced me to go back to the '90s, to all those boxes with files, but now, unknown to me, my light body co-founder was about to die at the same time. And he wanted me to stay alive. So he supplied energy. And he blessed the writing.

And he's a magnificent consciousness, with great guides behind him. So when I was sitting in his last seminars (remote)— nobody knew they were the last—what I was sitting there doing, as all that energy poured in of people taking the seminar and all the guides called in, I was writing this book. So it had all this energy behind it, going back to the 1990s but in the present. I don't even know what it says hardly myself. It's a gift to me too. When I finished the *Principia*, the last of the 1990s files and passages and notes brought into the present, I was thinking: *I don't have to write anything else. Actually I think I've fulfilled what I HAD to write.*

But then these little sparkle beings came, and you inspired me to ponder on the *Principia*. So somehow this post-*Principia* or "where do we go now?" started pouring into me. And you and I started talking, and I thought: *I'll plop it right into this new book.* I want to keep this book short because I can't afford another long book in audio. They're tremendously expensive. I have to go to Portland, Oregon, etc., for the recording You'll read your part in Suriname, I hope.

In these talks, I hope we're giving the *Principia* some way to get out there into people. It didn't have it.

JEF: The first thing I want to do is finish reading it. Every morning, when I'm able to, I do my own exercises. I start with Taiji but then go into a very deep level of consciousness and awareness. More than that. You could say shamanistic level—actually, Taiji is shamanistic in origin. What I experienced since reading the *Principia* is that the levels you're describing and which by reading I'm taking in, I can quickly include them in the physical and energetic experience of the book. And from there, of course, new insights are coming in.

MAH: There's energy in the book, of course. And you're able to detect it and to actually grasp how to use it. I just realized you're stepping it down because you're integrating it. And therefore in the book itself now will be your energy. So even energetically you're making it easier for the people who read it to absorb.

JEF: Something else is happening.

MAH: Something else is happening.

JEF: Yeah, yeah, definitely. I experienced it the second morning and also while I'm reading. In the beginning I could follow very quickly, but now I see where in the middle part I really have to absorb it. Again this morning I can see it's a matter of *incarnating* this energy—somebody has to do this; they have to really bring this into this matter and radiate it again into the larger field of consciousness, but now in a conscious way. I will definitely also bring this into my teachings in the Taiji and shamanistic sessions, and all this sort of thing.

To me, it is this domino—brick. You actually push one and a whole new structure is falling down, but actually it's arising, it's something opening up from the Universe. For me, anyway, the trigger point is the *Underground Principia*. It's really a fabulous work. We really have to dedicate ourselves more to it. I want to experience it. Especially the layers of electricity and so on, the things you were describing there. I will elaborate on that later.

Interruption MAH: "It's a gift. . . . For me too. Woooaaaaa. Early in the book, in the scene at the graveside, what did I see? People standing there, seeming to be bringing gifts. I had a clear picture of a solemn ceremony, as it were, of gifts being brought. So here we are. The scene is materializing. Incarnating itself. Fulfilling the picture of itself far into the future. From somewhere out there in the universe, the spirit world is bringing a gift. But I saw a number of gifts. Perhaps—let's assume—go with it—ALL these recent books are gifts. Each one brought individually. A group of spirits, each with a gift in hand. Wow. I knew it. But now Jef puts it into words, connecting his experience of a gift to the gift-laden delay of my death.

Returning to the Skype Chat

JEF: [Back to his experience in reading *An Underground PRINCIPIA*] Two things are happening: I can grasp it and

I can do something with it. But I wanted to share—because you questioned whether, actually it's the brain doing it. So these past days at an energetic and a very deep awareness level I was sensing this—for the moment I could connect to the electricity, as you said, and all this Life field—and I was drawn into the skeleton structure of my being because in my past I'd been doing these Tibetan exercises with Jóska, where we concentrate on the bone structure and so forth as part of a session, and I was really drawn into the bone structure of my being. *And suddenly I connected to the intelligence of the stem cells* because they're in all your bones, the stem cells. And it was so amazing that I could see no, the brain is only an *extension* of the stem cells. The real intelligence and the real sensitivity for this Life field is in our stem cells. And this is why they're protected so well in our skeleton.

ASIDE—INTERRUPTION. I questioned Jef later. What passages were the triggers?

JEF (identified them):

> These sequence of paragraphs / thoughts triggered me to go into depth regarding the stem cells communicating with the quantum field. Especially the last one.

> My search was how cells would recognize sister electricity . . .

> Chapter 4, pages 79 a.f.

> Gleick continues: *Clearly—or almost clearly—the brain does not own any direct copies of stuff in the*

world. There is no library of forms and ideas against which 80 to compare the images of perception. Information is stored in a plastic way, allowing fantastic juxtapositions and leaps of imagination. Some chaos exists out there, and the brain seems to have more flexibility than classical physics in finding the order in it.

Page 97

So I felt the back (or past) taken care of, and the present (or future) emptied, so that only nothingness was there. The nothingness even accompanied itself by periods of shutdown of my body, when the stillness created near-sleep that must have been in a brainwave deeper than theta, but without sleep. At this juncture, the soul deposited information, but directly to the cells. It was the only way.

Page 105

The theme jumped around through the image. As a matter of fact, just how? Because brains were involved. And what they got inspired by. Not that brains can breathe, inhale the germ, of the idea, that way, though they do need oxygen—but evidently they can take in perpetuated themes

Chapter 5, page 161

How long could we hide from the fact that "so we have electrical circuits in our brain, our body, electrical impulses—electricity is our 'message carrier'?" Did we think they would not recognize sister electricity out there in the universe or in its very viewing moment at, for instance, the television set?

MAH: You're making me think the stem cells are like the little bulbs that you plant—of the flowers—because they have the future in them, they have the intelligence in them.

JEF: Yes.

MAH: Are they *thinking?* . . . If it's not the brain, are they thinking?

JEF: It's not the brain. What I experienced is that actually, our stem cells—the intelligence in our stem cells—really connect to the most subtle part of this energetic field. This is why when you said that the future is already there . . . all this information is there . . .

MAH: Oh my goodness.

JEF: And they connect to it. They just use the whole nervous system. Also the brain.

MAI I: That's really deep, Jef, and then are they connecting to kundalini—if you want to bring in . . . it's called intelligent. It's never been explained, this intelligent energy, Mother Shakti. If you get down to that world, where there's all this intelligence and the kundalini's in our body, . . . it just makes me wonder.

JEF: [Jef is making a lot of gestures, very focused, at this point] There *is* a connection because from taking in this energy, they create the kundalini, they create the energetic structure.

MAH: Oh my goodness. Somewhere it had to be *created*, Jef, and nobody ever said where it was created. [Both are using gestures now, highly focused, as if Jef is still experiencing the experience.]

JEF: It's really coming from the combined intelligence of our stem cells. And it was such a deep experience—

MAH: You mean all the stem cells are working together in different—?

JEF: They connect to our intelligence.

MAH: No, but I mean not just inside your body, all the stem cells, but in all the bodies, do you mean the stem cells are communicating . . .

JEF: Inside my own body in connection with this larger field. Actually, we know for sure—this is common knowledge. Also, from all my students—that even the cells in our muscles cells, they soak up the energy from the environment and this is what we use to move around in martial arts, Kung Fu, shamanism. We bring ourselves inside this state of mind and then we transfer—you could say the vibration of the cell, the vibration of the energy of the body—it's an exchange of energy.

But *this* is on a much, much deeper level that I experienced.

This is the intelligence talking to this larger field. The stem cells are different from the other cells in our body. They have their own intelligence. *It was so amazing this morning.*

MAH: It's almost like a little being.

JEF: It *is* an entity.

MAH: It has to be if it's carrying all those thoughts or order. If it has awareness, or is it mechanical? It's awareness.

JEF: No, no, it's awareness. It's connected to the Light. This is awareness. They read the information coming from the larger field. Wherever it is coming from. But I mean on the most subtle level. The most subtle I can experience.

MAH: Are you still in contact with them?

JEF: Yes. Since this morning it's permanent in my body. This week, every morning, I went into a deeper state of mind, this really deep level of my body. And this morning it really hit me so strong.

MAH: What have I done to you, Jef?

JEF: It's good because I will look younger. [both are laughing]

MAH: You're looking younger. Your face has cleared.

So if you're thinking of incarnating, the stem cells can hold the energy to incarnate. What are you going to turn into, I wonder? It's just a form of you, but it's—

JEF: they really attract life force.

Light, and our life force. And what we call chi, or karma. They really attract it.

MAH: [half facetiously] So do your stem cells get unhappy? Do they say they are ready to kill you if you just—

JEF: In shaman tradition, one of the principles—now I'm just repeating what Jóska told me. One of the axioms is that it prolongs our life, and we rejuvenate while we are doing it. We can reach much more than the seventy-two, seventy-four, years of our average lifetime. One of the teachers in our Taiji school, Master Ni Hua Ching—the last time I heard from him, he claimed he was one hundred twelve. He was living in Taiwan.

ASIDE: Master Ni Hua Ching has a website in which, among other things, he has links to his translation of the *Tao Te Ching* and the works of Lao Tse as well as his interpretations of them.

The Universe Is a Big Piece of Energy. Human Life Is a
Small Piece of Energy.
The Big and the Small Share the Same Essence and Nature.
They Both Abide within the Subtle Law.
—Master Ni Hua Ching

Lao Tzu Did Not Initiate Taoism. He Was a Historian and
Librarian for the Royal Court. He Studied the Library
Materials and Also Had His Own Teachers. He Complied
His Learning into the *Tao Te Ching*.
—Master Ni Hua Ching

MAH: Dhyanyogi-ji lived to one hundred sixteen or seventeen.

114

JEF: To do this is to attract this level. I think it is a matter of attracting it—I'm very far from this level. But then it has to do with these exercises we are doing. Aligning. But then it connects to the kundalini, of course. And the tree of life. And it's aligning these three centers: the head center, the heart, the *dantien*, and activating those. What I'm seeing now by reading *An Underground PRINCIPIA*, going into all this larger field and all this information—there is a deep connection, to be able to connect to these three centers: the head, the heart, and the belly. And then our stem cells—it's actually our stem cells creating this deep energetic structure. And this creates the human being.

They are very very tiny cells. They really connect to the light. In my experience—what I experienced this morning—they are in fact photosynthetic cells; they are absorbing this light in our being. This is why they are guarded—they are protected so very well.

ASIDE: To my surprise, what did I stumble on a few weeks later? That stem cells had been the basis of a discovery fifty-six years before. *Fifty-six years!* To me, this looked now like a domino, in Jef's opening description.

Pioneer cell biologist Bruce Lipton, PhD, in his foreword to *The Science of Subtle Energy: The Healing Power of Dark Matter*, described his discovery of epigenetics: "As a young developmental biologist in 1967, I had the unique opportunity of cloning multipotential stem cells."

Starting from a single stem cell in a culture dish, Lipton derived about thirty thousand genetically identical stem cells. The single cell just kept dividing and those cells divided. Then, setting them into three Petri dishes, he gave a "specific growth medium" to each. He called the different dishes "environments": the laboratory equivalent of blood.

Following environmental signals, these three sets of genetically identical stem cells produced *different* gene expressions, "contradict[ing] the reigning central dogma of molecular biology, the belief that DNA is self-actualizing, being able to turn itself on and off in controlling biological life." That is, that it operates mechanically.

But Lipton's experiments led him in a different direction: "genes," he said, "did not control their own expression; genes were *being controlled* by information from the environment."

Thus, reaping scientific scorn.

Did other biologists listen?

No, "because they were imbued with the conventional belief that genes control their environment."

But, he said, his experiments demonstrated that "Much like Newton could predict the movement of planets, I was able to predict the results in my cell cultures." However the deaf ears heard not a believable sound in this line of thinking. Then, in 1990, in an unswift turn-around, "science established a new field, epigenetics." No longer did genes alone, set in a fixed line of expression, control our destiny. Science now "recognized the role of the environment in shaping genetic activity."

No, genes did not act mechanically. They met their environment and responded accordingly to the signals, which "could modify the readout of genes, without altering the genetic code."

Lipton says he is "recounting [his] personal story [there, in the foreword] because, today, [Russian scientist] Yury Kronn stands at the same point where I stood in 1967."

That is, in his replicable experiments with—what?—subtle

116

energy. Experiments that violate "the Newtonian concept of a universe containing two noninteracting realms, of matter and energy, which still dominates the current biological paradigm."

"The new physics, now almost a hundred years old, has yet," he explains ruefully, "to be fully adopted by biomedical science"; instead, it insists on treating matter as if "it can only be affected by matter."

So there you have it. What? Particles can be affected by something other than matter?

This holding tight by biomedical science onto the old way of thinking, dismissing effects of subtle energy on matter, comes despite the discovery of the tiniest of particles, "made of energy vortices and . . . not expressed as matter"! The universe is replete with them.

Name one.

The neutrino.

Hark and listen carefully. It is not true that—traditional medicine to the contrary—matter "can only be affected by other matter."

To again quote Einstein, Lipton says, " 'The invisible energy field is the sole governing agency of the particle (matter).' "

He goes on:

> Yury Kronn and others show experiments that are influenced by an unrecognizable energy realm they refer to as subtle energy . . .
>
> We cannot survive by continuing to follow the mission of science established in the 1600s by Francis Bacon, to control and dominate nature. The reason is we are not outside *observers* of nature, we *are* nature.

Fascinatingly, to me, he states:

> Consciousness is an energy that [as experiments show] does not dissipate over time and distance. While we are aware that electromagnetic waves become weaker over time and space, the energy in Kronn's experiments is not affected by distance and time. Consciousness is not an electromagnetic field . . .
>
> The observations in Kronn's research demand science to focus its attention on the role of subtle energies in shaping our world.[13]

So where does all this leave us? Hanging on the edge of our seats, I'd say. After this buildup in this book, I have merely copied down—spread the word on—a brilliant discovery recounted in another book?

No. I have stumbled on the same Discovery Mechanism.

Stem cells strike again. The fact that merely *having* a gene or gene sequence existing inside you does not predetermine the expression of that gene *in* you—a principle that Lipton eventually got recognized—took the spotlight, obviously. But looking underneath that, we find that this discovery came in through, what? A subtle energy system of its own.

It could have come in in any fashion. What it happened to come in through was stem cells. Which is not irrelevant to us. Is it? Lipton was concerned with how DNA receives environ-mental signals. A stem cell experiment gave him his answer. But here, with us, you and me, readers, stem cells jump into the fray. They are kinetic. The fact that passively they provided the platform for the earlier discovery now leads, in my trail, to subtle energy itself: that it is creating the trail. Isn't it?

118

The domino is yet larger. It is not a single revelation. We find something under that revelation. Let's see what. NASA Science tells us in "Anatomy of an Electromagnetic Wave":

> The terms light, electromagnetic waves, and radiation all refer to the same physical phenomenon: electromagnetic energy. . . . All three are related mathematically such that if you know one, you can calculate the other two. . . . Radio and microwaves are usually described in terms of frequency (hertz), infrared and visible light in terms of wavelength (meters), and x-rays and gamma rays in terms of energy (electron volts).

Is everything electromagnetic energy in various forms?

Impossible, as perhaps 95 percent of the universe is invisible "dark matter" and "dark energy." We have miniscule understanding of it. We do not know what it is. At all. We do not have that curtain pulled back. Is answering that question to take millions, billions of years? Or is revelation on a roll? Is it one of the dominoes now lined up? But we do know that it is *outside the electromagnetic spectrum*. It is NOT Light.

Dark matter, dark energy, is Not Light? Then what have light workers been doing all this time? Is it a misnomer?

The Science Mission Directorate of NASA picks up the thread in "Anatomy of an Electromagnetic Wave," calling energy "a measure of the ability to do work." Colorfully, the article distinguishes between "stored, or potential, energy" found in such things as "batteries and water behind a dam." And kinetic energy—i.e., of things in motion.. . .

Charged particles—such as electrons and protons—create electromagnetic fields when they move, and these fields transport the type of energy we call electromagnetic radiation, or light

> Mechanical waves and electromagnetic waves are
> two important ways that energy is transported in the
> world around us. Waves in water and sound waves in
> air are two examples of mechanical waves. Mechanical
> waves are caused by a disturbance or vibration in
> matter, whether solid, gas, liquid, or plasma.[14]

Dark matter pulls matter—galaxies, in fact—together, and dark energy comes right behind (or ahead of) it and pushes galaxies apart.

"In short," Eric Betz, explains (in What's the difference between dark matter and dark energy?"), "dark matter slows down the expansion of the universe, while dark energy speeds it up."

> Dark matter works like an attractive force—a
> kind of cosmic cement that holds our universe
> together. This is because dark matter does inter-
> act with gravity, but it doesn't reflect, absorb, or
> emit light. Meanwhile, dark energy is a repulsive
> force—a sort of anti-gravity—that drives the
> universe's ever-accelerating expansion.
>
> Dark energy is the far more dominant force
> of the two, accounting for roughly 68 percent of the
> universe's total mass and energy. Dark matter makes
> up 27 percent. And the rest—a measly 5 percent—
> is all the regular matter we see and interact with
> every day.[15]

Enough. We'll come back. This is a saga we are hot on the heels of as the dominoes stand revealed.

MAH [resumes the story of her sister having a cardiac arrest, setting it into a trio of life-threatening, extreme situations striking the three sisters. And why three? There is folklore about three in strong incidents. Whys? What was three historically? We'll skip except lightly].

Can particles count? I say that facetiously, but how can the three of us be lined up, in a life-threatening incident for each of us? Is it about patterns, and can patterns be lined up? Where would the inclination to make it three come from? (Or four, but my sister and her daughter almost count as one, they are so close.)

How does the universe count? Who's counting? It's not like my sister said: *I have to count.* Nowhere in her consciousness is there such a theory.

JEF: You know, the Celts were there, in Europe, long before the Romans invaded. In Celtic druidism, which is also shamanism, they say all things come in threes.

MAH: What do they mean by that?

JEF: From what I know, they say that every event has an anima, an animus, and can be androgynous.

MAH: So just to go along with that because you put it out there, I would be anima, my sister who came back with all that fighting male energy would be animus, and my third sister, who had an auto accident, totaling her car, would be androgynous. And what would then happen? We would be put into some kind of little collective energy?

JEF. That's what I took from your book. One of the principles is that you understand that events are actually meant to wake us up. In our "humanness." "Human," you know, is an extremely large field.

From my experiences I understand my humanness is not just a physical structure. So to get in connection with the event because from connecting with the event, I will understand my humanness. It's a matter of connecting the dots. A few years ago we started talking about synchronicity. It's not only in the moment. The thing from the past, the thing in the now, and the thing from the future—they are connected. And we have to connect the dots. The greatness of this field surrounding us and creating all the other things. And it happens with unpleasant things, but it also happens with the pleasant side.

The unpleasant is the physical side of it, but the pleasant is that you all came out very well. And there is some grace in that happening in those three moments. And understanding the grace is what creates our humanness.

MAH: I can feel the grace. It lifts everything up. We should be kind to other people too. That's the grace of it.

JEF: We become more human.

MAH: And human is changing all the time.

JEF: We don't even know the boundaries of human. At least, I don't know. Ever since I started connecting to the trees in our surroundings, thirty years ago, when I could dissolve into the forests, or in Corsica, when I jumped from that high rock into the *marquis* [heavy shrubs], you just connect to this larger entity. And what I experienced *this* morning is that this ability to connect is done by our stem cells. They bring us into this state where we can connect. And this kundalini, it's probably the highest state of this. It's pure bliss.

MAH: Naturally, if the stem cells are absorbing light, then they could connect to other stem cells, which are connecting to the light. The light body co-founder, his guide was DaBen, said consciousness begins when order begins, so anything that has organization to it—that would be everything that has life force—a little virus—anything that has organization—consciousness is there. It's not our consciousness, obviously. I connected it to what you said about its being aware of its environment.

JEF: The moment you were talking about order and how all these things contain life force, suddenly I saw these geometrical structures which Jóska always painted. He made like a hundred thousand of them. The light beings and the light structures that he painted—

One day he flipped like maybe two hundred pages in front of me and said"—forcefully—*"Just absorb. Just absorb. Just absorb."*

The lesson for that day was *"Just absorb."* But it reminds me, he also said, "The universe geometizes." Everything is in a certain order. And you see that also in the Flower of Life that people are using, with all these triangles. I think, again, this is an expression of this Celtic idea: they accepted this universal principle of the triangle shape of everything that happens. There must be these three primordial forces, to find the shape of everything that happens. In martial arts, why do we speak of these three primordial forces? Because we know the *dantien* connects to the world. The heart is the one that goes out. This is a centrifugal force. And the one in the head is the one that attracts the light; it's a centripetal force.

And when we are in these deep states we can see how the energy is settling there. In Taoist tradition, deep Taoist philosophy and meditation, they call these the god of the head, the god of the heart, the god of the *dantien*. They visualize them.

※

Moving on to Carl Jung:

> Chance events occur most often in larger or smaller series or groups . . . "It never rains but it pours." This proverbial wisdom is primitive science.

> "A woman I know was awakened one morning by a peculiar tinkling on her night-table . . . the rim of her tumbler had snapped off." She rang for another one. The same thing happened. She rang for another one.

> Within twenty minutes the rim broke again, with the same tinkling noise. Three such accidents in immediate succession were too much for her. She gave up her belief in natural causes on the spot and brought out in its place a primitive 'collective representation'—the conviction that an arbitrary power was at work. Something of

124

this sort happens to many modern people—provided they are not too thick-skulled—when they are confronted with events which natural causes fail to explain. We naturally prefer to deny such occurrences. They . . . disrupt the orderly course of our world and make anything seem possible, thus proving that the primitive mind in us is not yet dead.

Primitive man's belief in an arbitrary power does not arise out of thin air, as was always supposed, but is grounded in experience. The grouping of chance events justifies what we call his superstition, for there is a real measure of probability that unusual events will coincide in time and place.

—Jung, *The Earth Has a Soul* (108)

Sean Carroll, on YouTube, "A Brief History of Quantum Mechanics," makes a live experiment, sending a signal to Geneva, Switzerland, that, he says, just by the delivery of this signal establishes a new universe in which one him is different from another him that didn't respond to the signal or preceded it. But quantum mechanics is so complex, so difficult to understand, that no one tries anymore, he says. It's like the fox and the grape in Aesop's fable, where the fox learns that the grape is out of reach and says he never wanted it anyway. The fox is physics. Carroll disagrees and says we should learn to understand it.

Meanwhile, we have quantum computers that use qubits that can be in multiple states at the same time, or "superimposed." This makes computing with qubits enormously fast.

But what happens when these quantum-computing computers are turned on? When they spout out conclusions based on qubits, which can be not just 0 or 1 but both at once? In shock, NASA officials watched. In just a few days, quantum computing can solve what on even the largest-size classical computers "would take thousands of years." Also, a quantum computer exists, powered by only one photon, that is the size of a desktop PC.[16] Google said, in December 2024, "its quantum computer, [which] is based on a computer chip called Willow, needed less than five minutes to perform a mathematical calculation that one of the world's most powerful supercomputers could not complete in 10 septillion years, a length of time that exceeds the age of the known universe."[17]

In less than five minutes instead of 10 septillion years. I'll take that any day.

"The New Frontier in Oxytocin Physiology: The Oxytonic Contraction - PMC":

> According to the principle of "maximum parsimony" enunciated by Galilei, as Nature does not work with many things what it can operate with few" (dialogue concerning the two chief world systems, Galileo Galilei, 1632) means that every natural phenomenon is always realized with the minimum expenditure of both matter and energy. Its analytical formulation consists in the principle of minimum work.

So particles can exist in multiple states (can be super-positioned). What then?

What is often not pointed out is the discovery, by some of the early quantum mechanics physicists, the pioneers, that the ancient yogis were working in this field long before, but in an entirely different (observational) method they called yogic science.

First, though, what had to happen to these yogis?

They had to be in—a lifted vibration.

This was Law Number 1.

Ah, not in Western science. You could rush in after two hours of sleep—a big party the night before, hung over (though I'm not saying that ever happened)—and get to work. Didn't matter.

Compare that to a yogi "living" in an "awakened" state—night and day "holding the space," holding the focus, for the insights that dropped in.

A field based in observation—handed down over centuries—that was Yogic science which, by the way, some early Western QM giants felt affinity with. It included just what these Skype chats discuss—visions, inner observation, deep awareness, which these yogis passed on, often one on one to a single disciple.

Let's take an Overview plunge, turning to the Goswami Yoga Institute and Henrik Levkowetz (Sri Amit Goswami's disciple). From "Some Points of Comparison between Yogic Theory and Quantum Physics"

For a long time, theoretical physics was domi-nated by the principles of Newtonian mechanics.

Yes, yes, we know.

Let's go further into that article. The Newtonian principles, it tells us, state among other things that cause and effect are uniquely interrelated. Thus the same cause will always give the same result. Also, according to Newton's mechanics, the only limitations imposed on physical observations are the resolving power of the measuring apparatus. Thus by constructing finer and finer instruments, phys-icists rightly expected to get an ever expanding knowledge of Nature. They felt that there was nothing in principle that would prevent them from gaining the ultimate knowledge of the material world.

Centuries went by in this belief. The instruments, however, were having trouble keeping up, even as they got finer and finer.

But this author, Henrik Levkowetz, brings up a very interesting point about the quantum theory. In his own words: "*Now more than ever, the development of physics depends on a suitable development of scientists' intellectual abilities.*"

However, that's not where the focus of quantum mechanics is today, he reminds us. It's very intent on resolving the conflict arising over the incompatibility between quantum mechanics and Einstein's gravitation theory of general relativity—two camps reflecting the views of the famous QM pioneers Niels Bohr and Albert Einstein—Bohr coming down on the side of our inability to "know beforehand," as he put it, "with 100% certainty the effect of a certain cause." To give some background on that, in case you don't know, here's how the article puts it. According to Bohr:

We are never certain which side will turn up [in a coin flip when the coin] lands, but we know by experience that each side will show up in 50% of the cases ... *Contrary to this, Einstein expressed the belief that the microcosm too, is governed by strictly deterministic laws. . . . His principal view may be expressed by citing one of his typical remarks in this connection: "God does not play dice." But what is it then that makes our observations of the microcosm indeterminable?* To observe something, we have to use our senses and, in many cases, some scientific apparatus as well. *However, . . .*

Here is the key. If you were "asleep" before on this page, reader, wake up right at this point. You will realize a major fact. If you want to believe your meditations bring "real" knowledge and why—hark right here:

we always need a certain small amount of physical energy to activate our sensory receptors. When we observe a microcosmic system, the energy of the system might be of the same order of magnitude as the energy involved in the act of observation. So, by observing the system, we change it, and therefore we cannot tell how the system would behave without the interference of the observation. In this way uncertainty is always introduced by the act of observation. The finer the observed object, the more uncertainty will be introduced into the observed data. (my italics)

Compatibility With Yogic Theory

Many aspects of Quantum theory are consistent with yogic theory. *Yogic theory clearly states that there is a limit to the knowledge that can be attained in the sensory way. Above a certain level, indicating the subtleness of the phenomenon involved, it is not possible to perform sensory observations.* This level, technically called the *anu* 1) level, apparently corresponds in some way to the energy involved in the act of observation. [However,] the knowledge of the rishis has not come from physical experiments and mathematical analyses, *but by practicing Yoga to elevate their minds above the sensory level.*[18]

So there you have it—the stark difference. The reality of one is the illusion of the other—or at least impossible to "prove." Yogis do not operate in laboratory-style "proof." But by attaining information—how? By being in a higher state of consciousness, which we now know involves a shift in brain waves and what we, in the West, measure as brain "coherence."

(In contrast, many leading scientists do not recognize a world outside the physical.)

But wait! After piling experience on top of experience for centuries, the yogis' view of reality is no longer conjecture. At least, to early QM, mystical-sympathizing pioneers. Or to me. Why?

Back to this article from Henrik Levkowetz (the Goswami Yoga Institute website): Microsoft Word - Quantum Physics Theory & Yoga Theory.doc:

They [these evolved yogis] are thus able to experience a quite different world on a super-sensory level, and then come back to the sensory level again, aware of the difference . . . They will then be able to formulate their knowledge (to a certain degree) in language for the information of those who cannot go beyond the sensory level . . .

How to Proceed Henceforth?

What can be done to proceed further in the science of microphysics, a.k.a. atomic physics?

The answer: a) "a reduction of the energy involved in the act of observation," b) "an enhanced intellectual power on the parts of the scientists . . . The ability to make refined measurements on atomic systems is ever increasing, *but as the absolute limit is approached, the difficulties of retrieving information from experiments on microcosm is also increasing*." (my italics)

Back to Levkowetz:

> However, according to Yoga, there is another method of developing the consciousness beyond the sensory level. This consists of bringing the mind immediately above the intellectual level by the practice of mental concentration. Here, at the so-called *dhi* level, the mind is focused on the object of meditation to such an extent that all reasoning will cease. By regular practice, the power of reasoning will be enhanced when the mind is back on the ordinary level . . .

Hatha Yoga is only one example of the routes to expanding consciousness: In the *suprasensory states, "as no material energy is involved, the limitations treated by Quantum Theory do not apply."*

So here is the point. At the Goswami Institute they know that yogic findings—in deep states—go beyond physical energy.

And then what?

"All reasoning ceases." With reasoning displaced, there it is, coming in on a different vibration. *Knowing*. Problem solved. You cannot be "told" about it. It's experiential. The institute admits that it's not easy: To sum this up: science recognizes only "brain-related consciousness." Not so, says yoga:

> The brain, according to Yoga, is not a consciousness-generating organ, but rather a reducing factor of a more encompassing consciousness. If consciousness somehow is liberated from the limitations produced by the brain, it is then possible to surpass its usual sensory limits and access a broader consciousness. We need both the higher consciousness to clearly see the solution to the problems we face during ordinary, karmic-regulated human life, and ordinary consciousness endowed with the individual's power to cope with these problems.

All this I have said many times. The ancient yogis and their traditions handed down, sometimes from master to only one student, recording it mentally or in the subtle energies or written down in some primitive manner, consciousness principles—some of which were seized upon independently by their counterparts in QM later, in the nineteenth and twentieth centuries, long after the yogis started building their so-named "yogic science," which fulfills some, but not all—by any means—of the requirements of "science" in the West.

Why not go first? I always say? Anyone want to keep going in building up this edifice that started revealing itself, with the crashing down of the first domino?

But here a principle I wasn't aware of enters in. *If physical energy is used, as in measuring in a laboratory, then that energy affects the experiment, creating an ultimate limitation. This, we know. Stop here, science.*

What if, in reaching a different brain state, *you get beyond this limitation?*

There, yogic science—not knowing the issue existed, because it didn't at the time—waited for this scientific need for it. For centuries it was transmitting, with or without directly intending it, these frequencies far and wide. So far that they came right over to the West. And out beyond the planet.

Of course they did.

There, in the East, though, it waited. What do you think, Jef? If we just hop back in to where our Skype meet was going, my question magically happens to fit in. Well, at least a bit.

Reading the manuscript, Jef commented that, importantly, this text relates to the Seven Spheres of Consciousness, which are described in the appendix, at the end of this book.

JEF: Biographies tell us, we also have to understand, that the first impulse for a new discovery or a new insight, it is always a vision, whether it is Archimedes shouting Eureka or Einstein seeing photons in his tea as he saw the sugar melting while stirring the tea—it made him understand something about photons. It always starts with an image. A feeling, actually.

MAH: Where on earth did you read that about Einstein?

JEF: I read it when I was fourteen years old and started to take interest in quantum physics. I do not remember the book but I do remember clearly this event the author described.

MAH: I guess it came spontaneously because of his habit of having thought experiments he put in visual terms.

MAH: When they understand it with their brain, then to turn it into mathematics.

And now this:

Is AI Taking Control of Our Thoughts? Researchers Warn About the Emerging "System 0"[19]

Nobel laureate Daniel Kahneman's groundbreaking work on cognitive processes identified two primary modes of thinking : System 1 (fast and intuitive) and System 2 (slow and deliberative). However, recent research published in *Nature Human Behaviour* suggests the emergence of a third mode - System 0.

System 0 represents an **externalization of reasoning** facilitated by AI technologies. This new cognitive pathway allows humans to delegate complex data processing tasks to artificial intelligence systems, potentially augmenting our mental capabilities. However, it also raises concerns about our growing dependence on these external cognitive resources.

What is the result of this "cognitive offloading?

That's a no-brainer. Easy to figure that out.
But let's put the good things aside.

> System 0 represents an **externalization of reasoning** facilitated by AI technologies. This new cognitive pathway allows humans to delegate complex data processing tasks to artificial intelligence systems, potentially augmenting our mental capabilities.

But—researchers warn of possible downsides if humans lazily give their capacity for solution-making to AI. Then what?

• Over-reliance on AI-generated solutions
• Diminished capacity for independent thought
• Reduced ability to develop innovative ideas
• Potential amplification of existing biases

AN ASIDE:

"What You Can Learn from Einstein's Quirky Habits"

> More than 10 hours of sleep and no socks—could this be the secret to thinking like a genius?

> Newton . . . bragged about the benefits of celibacy. When he died in 1727, he . . . left behind 10 million words of notes; he was also, by all accounts, still a virgin (Tesla was also celibate, though he later claimed he fell in love with a pigeon) . . .

Many of the world's most brilliant scientific minds were also fantastically weird. From Pythagoras' outright ban on beans to Benjamin Franklin's naked "air baths," the path to greatness is paved with some truly peculiar habits.

But what if these are more than superficial facts? Scientists are increasingly realising that intelligence is less about sheer genetic luck than we tend to think. According to the latest review of the evidence, around 40% of what distinguishes the brainiacs from the blockheads in adulthood is environmental. Like it or not, our daily habits have a powerful impact on our brains, shaping their structure and changing the way we think.

"How Einstein Unlocked the Quantum Universe and Created the Photon" - Universe Today

Einstein discovered photons. You always hear, "Einstein discovered the photoelectric effect." But what does that mean? He discovered photons. Ah, clear.

He supposed that light itself was quantized. In other words, what we perceive as sloshing, undulating waves of electricity and magnetism is really, at a deeper, more fundamental level, a flood of discrete, distinct, indivisible little bundles of light-stuff. Each one of these bundles represents the smallest amount of light-stuff that you can possible have. And because these bundles are uncuttable, you cannot have fractional proportions of light-stuff.

136

. . . Electrons need a certain amount of energy
to get away from a metal. And that energy [is
determined by]—?

Its frequency.

Now that we have all that explanation behind us, let's go
on with Jef. The same chat. You see how these texts just fit in.
I haven't looked ahead. I am just playing a game—*speculating
it will fit. One way or another be an interesting juxtaposition.*

JEF: I said a discovery—whether it is Archimedes shouting
Eureka or Einstein seeing photons in his tea or whatever—it
always starts with an image. A feeling, actually. Then they
start to verbalize it and then they turn it into mathematics.

MAH: I would guess some people go straight to mathematics.

JEF: Bach with music. He did this.

But actually, the real—I can't say start because the start is
somewhere we don't know. But a new theory always starts
with only a feeling. I have a *feeling* about this. And then the
person direct the intention in this direction. *Only then* the
vision arises. Something touches the heart, and from the
heart something has to go out again into this large field of
electricity, this light field. And then the image—in a dream, a
vision, or whatever—but something will come.

MAH: I'm getting something that's important—to me
anyway. When we started studying light body, we were told
there were embedded transmissions in the guided meditation journeys that if we went back later, we'd get. But that

we didn't get earlier. That's the way the light body worked, with embedded transmissions. They were general but could be targeted to a person. So—this sounds crazy, but it's what I really think—if there are embedded transmissions in the book, these stepping stones to get out in the world—the embedded transmissions will be like little parachutes. I've had people put their hand on my book, then say,. *Now I don't have to read it.*

But this is more: not just energy people can find there. If you have energy transmissions accessible when you listen to (originally) cassette tapes, then the CD form, now downloads, you can obviously put them into a book. It would be this specific process that was going on in light body. You've just shown me that. I didn't get it till now. The same process. How fascinating. Thank you. Yeah. Hmmm. That's fascinating, the whole thing.

I'm going to type up everything that's relevant that we say. But there's much that's not.

JEF: It was the same already in my military career ("How did you acquire these states?" "I don't know. By intuition. An innate capacity of absorbing delicately the information or the energy we need.")

MAH: That potential, you have. But more than that, it existed out in the universe. But you have it. And some other people have it, like Jóska. It's a capacity, but most of the billions of people don't know they have it. I remember this Indian just before he became formally a guru. He said *there's no point in writing books.* But I see now how—if you can turn it—

Multimedia is going on now in the web. Well, *this* [embedding transmissions] is multimedia—if you can embed processes, energies, whatever, into this book—

Not just energy but specific transmissions and targets. Before Duane started teaching he worked as a geophysicist; he had a PhD in geology/geophysics. He started going into Sanaya Roman's energy classes. For a year after work he attended in his business suit, not saying a word; walked to the front of the class and when it ended, just left, not saying a word. And what he was doing, he was calling his students. So when the time came to teach, they appeared from everywhere. I came from Belgium. My light body teacher, who was in Belgium, would fly to the US. How did he hear about it? Because DaBen was using the energy of the class. He didn't just do it in his room. He went into the class, using the energy. And called the students. And everywhere—nearby, other places like China and Holland—how could people hear about his class? Because he gave a call. So I'm saying you could do this kind of thing in a book.

JEF: I can fully accept your idea. [He explains about meeting a Belgian politician, who convinced him to write a book, *Eternal Spring*, about his ecological ideas.] He was incorruptible. I was talking to him about a flaw in Belgian politics. He invited me to his home and we spoke for a day; then I had this idea to write my ideas down. First, for working groups to redesign this political landscape. He was the most highly decorated politician in Belgium. [Long story short] Two years later, suddenly this thought comes: *Now you're going to write this book about ecology*—I said to myself: *Why am I doing this? I don't want to do it. I don't want to be involved with politics. Leave me alone.* In a few weeks I wrote *Eternal Spring*. My wife asked, "What are you doing?" "Never mind, I just have to do it." And what I was doing was creating a framework: "This is s line you can follow."

MAH: That gave him what he needed.

JEF: Yes. And the only thing I had to do was *write* that book. People around me from the NGO, eco systems in Belgium, said, "No, no, no. We have to publish it and go around—" I said, "No, I don't want it. I only have to write this book. I only have to *reorganize this energy*." Which is exactly what you are saying.

By doing it, it creates a new energy. You are bringing it into an action in writing it down. It will disperse again. It will go into the universal field again." So I fully subscribe to this idea that by writing a book, you can teach—

MAH: You give this widely dispersed thought a form. Like an event has a form. So then it can have that to stand on and encounter. Have force and impact that way. Otherwise, it was too dispersed. Lost its ability to have an impact. Thus, to have any meaning. It could not have *any encounters*. Until it had some sort of existence. Was in a form, like you say.

JEF: You can sit *right there* and say, "I'm teaching light body."

Yes, by writing these things down.

This is why I can grasp the energy and practice it here in the jungle. Whatever you are writing, I can grasp the energy.

MAH [realizing the implications, unthought-of mediums]: You are saying that light body teachings I experienced can go into the book, my *Underground PRINCIPIA*; that—Duane blessed my writing and he's not here, teaching in person—that it can go, targeted and with transmissions, into a book—if I dare tell myself that. That's fabulous. I can hardly bring myself to see it. *But it's not about me.*

JEF: We're just instruments. The Light is moving us.

MAH: Yeah, that's it. It's the Light. And if you put yourself in, the Light isn't interested.

JEF: The Light *might* be interested in you. [A laugh]

It's interested in us.

MAH: The Light's interested in everyone.

So then that's why this current book started. I had to have your interest in it to start transforming it. Stepping it down. And stepping it up. From there, this new book, which starts after the 1990s files are gone—I don't go back at all. It's starting now. Some of the stories do go back but understood now. And then synchronicity comes in. And then anything we say now that's evolving out of the *Principia event* goes into the book. The energies are doing it. It's blowing my mind. It's beyond my mind. It's a decision I didn't make.

JEF: But it's a question from deep within you.

MAH: Yeah.

JEF: Although we don't make the decision, the answer is coming.

MAH: Yes. "Do not go gently into that dark night" . . . I wouldn't have liked having no more books to write. That is, not being the instrument. I wouldn't be getting new material I had no concept of, totally surprising me, coming in. Writing it down.

JEF: That's the mathematics of it . . .

MAH: Wow. The whole thing is amazing [at a loss for words]. Good heavens. I thought I was tired, coming into this conversation. And you threw me off my feet. It's so amazing, the things you're saying. And then I have these responses that come to me, through the vessel. It's amazing.

JEF: It's amazing for me as well.

＊

What is sinking in deeply is the inevitability of it, the "planning"—or intent—that goes "way back." And this realization that like one thing sitting on top of another, the practice, or method, of putting transmissions into cassettes (or however they are accessed by playing the cassettes—even turning the sound off) is repeatable in a book. And not just "a" book—this is *my* book we are talking about. *My books*, which didn't get much outside attention. And now that the "gift" has come, we are specifying that the *Principia* is carrying on, in its own way, the legacy of the light body course I've been taking, by couching the energies, in transmissions there. Where did the transmissions come from? Were they already embedded in the cassettes, the minds of DaBen and Duane targeted for this book back then? The pile of instants on instants, events on events, that extended? That far back in "time"? Did, the moment I set foot into class, "the book" begin "calling" to me to capture the energies for it? That's just one way of putting it. But was time reaching down and enacting the Plan? Then?

And then, of course, being human, I ask why me? I even shrink into my shell and say: "No, that makes me sound important. I don't dare put it that way."

But that's interference. Interference creates collapse. It means I have to go back and learn this lesson. That, God forbid, the experience will be "taken away from me." *No!* I shriek. *I am ready.*

So, again, an "energy call" is Light making contact, and not signaling that one person is more than another, but that that person fits this circumstance and perhaps has been being set up for it for years and decades, in human time. Maybe from the moment of planning to incarnate! Would you cancel out the purpose of your incarnation???!!!!

Just hammer this into your head. You are not to interfere.

Ah. I sigh a deep breath.

A new "me" has come in. It is Focus. Focus is suddenly my identity. That and nothing else. For now.

Focus knows who it is. It knows, penetrating out into Awareness, its name, its history. I don't. I identify with it. It is me. I know it. Isn't it in my mind? Didn't it peer through my mind when I was seven? I can handle it now. It's an easy step. Into Focus.

I, Paul—I keep saying that, trying to stay. But it doesn't matter.

The prophecy vision, the life plan, seen by me, Margaret, in being transported, in a kundalini kriya experience, immediately finding myself in an upper chamber to pick—as if it was only a matter of saying the word—a life identify: not plan, but "who" I would be. And how is that option possible?

But first, let's clear out all this gibberish, this side-talk. It may be useful somewhere else. But it prevents my being here. You know, again, the straightest distance to two points. Well, you have to use a straight distance to get to me. If you start inter-mixing in other thoughts, I disappear. Once again. So tell me again about the vision in which *you* "chose" *me*. I like to hear it.

—the vision I saw, of which "me" (or not exactly "me")—

Yes, that's the intriguing part. What's the relationship between your choice and "you"? Also, before/after.

I don't need to know. All I have to know is the answer—the choice—it has to be carried through sometime. So let's use this strength from long ago, with the Feminine to support. Just say, the Great Feminine.

You can't just "march in."

You can't? Anyway, maybe it will all remain a secret. Anybody can march through universality "in."

You think so? How?
By focus and awareness
You wanna bet?
Well, we're trying this. Let's keep on with it.

The focus is my friend. I am it. I want it to stay. It is as determined as the Little Dot I once saw, out of body, over my head. It IS that same focus. The feminine of it.

YES?

Well, we'll go with that. Not that it matters. Focus keeps sensing. Deepening. Straight out of one dimension into another. Deepening. Here?

Well, that was easy. Am I here?
Who are you?

The energies the Focus collected, gathered up—of You. Those ready to come here.

You are welcome. Come in.

What now?

Just wait.

We came to give you strength to stand up for yourself.

But I do.

Not enough for now. Now you will be asked to do bigger things. You must be in Focus so strong it is without question. It reaches to the Answer you expected. Why you came. Why I am here. Why I rushed over to add to the energy.

OK. I'm going to bed.

Being universal, I am "part of all that I survey."

Whitman?

Perhaps. So then, to get back to the thought descending into me, if energy can be deposited—transmitted—into cassettes (made so that wherever it "actually" is, or isn't but like particles that come into a location are "there" but not "there"), it can come alive as a person listens to the cassette or reads a book, if the person makes contact. That's the point: to "make contact."

Do you mean you could be "embedded" somewhere. But how suspenseful, not knowing where you'd be found.

Oh, but I knew. It takes a lot to "find" me. To go into universality and come back not so blissed out as to bring something like a human form with you.

❋

[Going back to the conversation on transmissions, messages, potential shifts, being embedded in a recorded spiritual journey, now, it turns out, they can be recorded in a memory put into a book.]

So can they likewise be deposited from person to person? Who are you? St. Paul? His energy? Deposited? Could it be deposited in the vision I had of choosing this incarnation life focus, "who" to "take"? And I had only to access the memory in the vision—which is a big "if," a big demand? For otherwise anyone reading the description of the vision could access it.

And could they? Can they? Is "he" up for grabs, that way?

Well, I'd better hurry. And get there first, to the energy left in a hiding place for me.

(So the playful part of the "large me" kept on. Sent down here and eventually recognized—as my Earth "Voice." No other way would anyone listen to me. Imagine if I started spouting generalities of abstraction. No, she did not speak that way. She did not know how. She "played.")

But the depth probe goes deeper, into another exact match. It hit a new synchronicity, made me stumble on it twenty-three years later—like finding a needle in a haystack. Helping Jef with his "White Crow manuscript," I came across a passage—really landed flat on my face—an explanation given to him by Master Po, a Taiji master. So this next synchronicity reaches me *from Taiwan!* Barreling across time and space. I am flabbergasted. The "depth charge" strikes. Master Po explained:

> "During the disembodied state—for most people, the state between death and a new birth—we experience our connection with the Great Breath much more intensely. Unless you learn to connect with it already in this life," and his gentle smile and the radiance in his eyes emphasized the power of this statement. "In that state, we understand our connection with all beings and that we are a link in the great cycle. From that knowledge, we create a dream for the next life. That dream is like answering a specific question.

What? "Answering a specific question?" I can't speak. My heart is thumping.

> You must find the answer to it during your life. Then you also do what you dreamed

of when you were in the Great Breath. That is
the fulfillment of your life. The answer to your
personal question is also an answer for all of
humanity and for the entire cycle. That is why it
is so important that you carry out the task you
have chosen during your life.

But this matches my kundalini kriya experience of
seeing myself, before birth, choose this lifetime focus—presented to me as a question. Amazing. As the Above, hovering,
zooming in, matches something Below, the energy tells me
it has struck the target, the match is real. I am receiving new
information about that kundalini episode, not in kundalini,
this time just in Awareness.

In the Gibran portrait of Mary Magdelaine inside
his book *Jesus Son of Man*, Jesus asked, "What would you,
Miriam?" In 1991, as I was recounting above, I was brought
up short, reading that essay. I heard, "Her water broke"
accompanied by an onset of kundalini kriyas that sent me to
an Upper Room where a small group sat around a table, and
one asked me who I chose.

So the question asked by Jesus bored through time, to
reappear in 1991, in California, as—not "What would you?"
but "*Who* do you choose?" Presumably in' 39 or '40, just
before conception. But the significance of the question *form*
didn't sink in, didn't have a peg to hang on. "What would
you, Miriam?" led eventually to Master Po, *just now*, making
me identify *for me* the moment of establishing "my dream."
My purpose. Hanging on that question.

Not only that. In receiving permission, I was told I had,
therefore, additionally to "take" Mary Magdalene. But how
complex. Like the event-combinations and reseedings spoken of

earlier. Two people, two consciousnesses, the Great Masculine and the Great Feminine. As if it was possible to step into two identities, from the past—or how we interpreted them, added to, handed down stories of? I "saw" nothing further, a quick snapshot of the moment of choosing: no explanation of what that meant. Just saw myself unhesitatingly answer "my question."

But it entailed two people whose consciousness those at the table must have been close to. How long was the list of choices? How short? How drawn up? I chose, somehow knowing who was in the list. For a list, it must have been. That was the way I answered the question.

But I was "dropped down" into the womb, missing this information. A moment so solemn, the memory of it brought back in such a way—it could not but be critical. And, more, a few years later—I had a second memory, in meditation (recorded elsewhere), in what I called an "energetic moment," taken this time to feel, right down on the particle level, relived, the instant St. Paul was struck by light on the Road to Damascus. Kundalini does not make these errors. It is strategic. It acts with things "in mind, superposed till it strikes down on us—it reinforces our choice. It bursts open to tell us what it is. Another most holy of holy moments. Then erased from my memory for the first half of my life, then revived. But in circumstances that didn't bring a context, therefore made it impossible to speak of it or even figure out "how" you "did" it. But maybe that was the point.

※

Hello. Here is the hiding place. Look. The awareness is looming stronger. Overwhelming me. Throwing me out? Is it only Awareness now, and who is "I"? Who? Going forth?:And shall we keep this secret?

Keep a process a secret? Not with me around.

Who are you?

The energy coming in with this "secret." The energy of universality's principles. Sweeping your consciousness out of the way.

So it's the return of the plan to "just walk in," that I had in a vision before and didn't at all put into practice. Had no idea how to or who would be walking in. Or what?

The plan sweeping its beacon light around to find companions to "just walk in" with.

Do they exist?

You don't even need to know about them, remember. Just Do, and you set it in motion. It has structure.

But suppose the "wrong" people pick this structure up.

Well, everything carries risks. Don't worry about it. Keep going to find out more.

And "just walk in" can be internal, you know. Then see what the "walk-in You" has in mind, in store, come to do. Even if just to you. Remodeling, molding. You will see.

Well, that was fun. Is any of it true? Am I playing a game to "pass the time"? Let's go on and see. But the Awareness state is real. It's hovering. I can let it take the place of my mind. I can rise to it, as to a UFO hovering just overhead. An awareness state, is that a UFO transporter, just that I can't see it physically? Perhaps it has a physical form I can't see.

And is exchanging that for you?

Yes.

The way it used to sit in my dantien?

Yes, or not quite. Sitting in the *dantien*, it was "weight," mass, but not so much. It could come and go, measurable on a scale but not a takeover of the mind, like this. It could sit quietly, unnoticed in the *dantien*. Sometimes. Always present but sometimes receding from the physical. When Awareness "sinks in," like this, there's a chance it will hang around longer, more consistently. Or consistently. It's listening to these talks.

So it can happen to the reader too? Deepening awareness by reading?

Or entering the Presence of the energy. Through the book. Or just as if walking into a room, by walking near the book, attuning the mind, the consciousness. Attunement is all.

So much happens just like that?

152

Just like that. The energy to attune to. You can "attune."
So this is part of the teaching of St. Paul.
Yes. He is a master "Attuner."
Ha.
You scoff.
I'm not scoffing. Marveling, more like. Thrown back on my heels taking a break from being lifted into the Awareness, identifying with it. Well, can everyone do that? Everyone who attunes to the energy.

To some degree. But there's also the Focus that's Yours, each individual.

There's that word. I thought this was universality we're in.
And cannot you be inside universality and focus here, then there? With training, yes. This Focus is holding massive energy. Composed of it. With training, you can enter it. Stepping in, you can faint in astonishment and refusal to let so much go. That keeps people out. They cannot accept the implications. Where is the personal me? Or you can sink into the energy and see where it wants to go. And WHO you then "are."
Oh, gosh.
Stop dividing yourself.
Step in. Disappear.
And so the chariot of Elijah enveloped me. And I was gone. No more.
Not a trace? Then who's here.
The reader, not yet reading, is speaking up. I am here. Let me go next.

"The Light might be interested in you," he said, with a big laugh. And so the next chapter descended. Those were not idle words.

BACK TO JEF:

MAH: It's not just writing books. It's being the instrument. Or I wouldn't be getting *new* stuff that I had *no* concept of, totally surprising me, coming in.

JEF: That's the third step, writing it down. The first step is that we experience it . . we have a deep impression. I cannot even talk about this deep impression—it's deep in my bone structure—I cannot talk about what it does to me: but there's all light in my being now. Then I can start to explain it and write it down: translate it to others.

MAH: It's the mysteries of the universe being revealed and shared. You cannot make them happen in any way. They come with the Light as a Gift.

※

This gift, superposed, overlays the other gifts, those in front of my would-otherwise-be death, blocking out the tombstone— the tombstone overshadowed by a "block" of guides, or spirits, or entities alive on Earth and off. Like coming to celebrate a birth. Or like ushering me to safety, en masse, out of a deadly situation. Silent. Somber. Intent. *Knowing.*

※

In what way is life—your life—like the seed you plant and then cared for it but finally don't have the decision-making power about whether it survives or not? Spirituality groups bring in here what they call "the law of attraction." We've lifted out Newton's perplexity about "attraction"—*what* is

154

the explanation why all particles of matter, though he didn't know about quantum particles—connect to each other?

Then, of course, which attractions hold? Which turn into luck and which disaster?

And what about that " "thin wire between survival and disaster"? What about "readiness is all"? It's not a new thought.

This is at the crux of the book. Over to you, Jef. I recently heard someone express astonishment at the unfolding of apparent happenstance in Hunter Thompson's life—surprise at how his achievement "did not *have* to happen" but for a series of accidents, near-mishaps, near fatally opposite choices that illogically took him to the originating point of Gonzo Journalism. But every step was a flip of the coin.

I answer, however, the companion of luck is risk.

Did things necessary to a certain result, "have to happen"?

Is that a basis of how Life works? A hidden variable, as it were? Is it "particles choosing"? Is it ourselves recognizing ourselves??????? Willing to take the risk to get to ourselves? Get to our purpose, or not? What is a quality of authenticity? So we have to have a certain amount of courage to be ourselves as it barrels toward us, or "get to" ourselves? Have to buck the mainstream, likely, because "we" are not there, "we" are in some obscure, obtruded position, finding the Light in it, working ourselves out of the perhaps-darkness there, or opaque surroundings, that partly reveals itself to us, but so iffy, so concealed as to outcome, we have to "see" or "sense" where it's taking us. Or just <u>might</u>.

I summarize this/lay out my thoughts for Jef. But it turns into an inner dialogue. So, first:

155

MAH: When somebody recently began to describe serendipitous events in Hunter's life story as a one-off, it brought to mind my discussion with Jef about people being *moved to meet.* That underneath happenstance the "had to happen" was at work.

I was astonished that anyone (not me) could think it was a principle in life that anyone could "plan" and "make" things happen. For uncertainty is inherent, at least in the human mind. We can sense the vibration of opportunity. We can know to "stop and look closer here"—the pull of the future outcome pressing upon the present. Some people push away the sensing device. But some people jump.

I have to again and again tell myself, "It's not about you." And maybe, as Jef said, "the Light is interested in you, Margaret." What?

Inside, I will believe it. My logical self will point out the evidence. But personally speaking, my ego may be shushing that voice. The emotional self, saying, *How could that be? No, it could not be.* And the logical self keeps running percentages and numbers and keeps coming up with the prediction. *The Light is interested in you. This is Light at work, moving you into position.*

"No," I "pretend" to respond, to myself. But more deeply. I'm saying: "Yes, yes. I cannot deny it. Why? I cannot know."

Not know? Oh, go deeper still.

And then I wind up in my experiential evidence. My most private, not-to-be-revealed kundalini experiences. They must mean something, no?

No, responds now my this-is-about-me self, gauging my size, as if it could, my unseen purpose, my "place" in this moment. For my logical self and even my personality are willing to accept the evidence, the way it is at least pointing, give that direction, that interpretation, a try. But what I thought was me says: *You cannot think like that.*

Woooossss. Cannot follow my thoughts?

No, delusion, self-propping up. And then the clincher: *What will people think?*

So it's gotten into my intuition—that karma, that old, worn-threadbare pattern.

No, this is a false intuition and you know it. Your true intuition is pointing the way, full steam ahead, with the logical self concurring.

But the flaw is that I say next: "What does it mean? What does it imply? How high up must that make me!?"

And this is the error. I cannot know. At this point. The end point. The Omega that is steadily pulling me.

You do not know how things work on this level?

Right. We are approaching universality; I do not know how things work there, which is like saying how things work in a pool of particles, moving around, with nary a hint (to us) what the decision will be, which will "fall" into an event on the Earth. And do they know? Is it happenstance there? Ah. Which gets chosen where?

I do not know how the "pool" of universality divides out its portions. How it supports focus. But the whole universe gets behind a "point." I have said that. Jef has said that. It also, however, gets behind a contradictory point. Universality lives in squaring that circle. Or leaving it unsquared. I can just follow the experiences that add up—if I am the one adding up. The facts that contribute. I cannot know, simultaneously, all the positions universality is sup-porting. And—ah-ha. Suppose it is like the Wolfgang Pauli exclusion principle where no two fermions (originally just electrons in Pauli's formulation) can occupy the same position at the same time.

This law says—let Wikipedia help out—"two or more identical particles with half-integer spins (i.e. fermions) cannot simultaneously occupy the same quantum state within a system that obeys the laws of quantum mechanics." What qualifies as a fermion? A wide range of particles, elementary and composite.

Ah, that would do it. The universe respects position. It is *positioning me*. It positions *us all.*

But right now I only know how it is positioning me. Not why. Not whether I "deserve" this or that. Not think in terms of exclusivity. Just follow the bouncing ball, the trail of breadcrumbs, the urging of the vibrations, the energy turning into—?

Apparently, the Mass of me.

The Energy of "E" marching into me, with the blessing of c^2.

Enough already. That was an outpouring, deluging the readers, who have many stories of their own. Many applications. Speak.

Well, historically, it's easy to pull up examples. There is one thing clear and certain, though. At any point in time, we did not walk around, giving two people the exact same identity. We even went so far as to say they could exist only one time. One spot, in the whole history of humanity, and on one planet, earth. So what did they do the rest of their "time," if they existed forever??? Did they come back, inside other energy? If the pool of energy repooled, if we selected our focus with it at our back, were we just renaming the same energy in new combinations—often.

Again, St. Paul stepped up. Look over here. I have been waiting, miniscule. In fact, it's not just up to you. Do I think you are "ready"?

November 24, 2024—with Jef

Well, it wouldn't be interesting today. My mind was far from this chat. I went into it, expecting the conversation to lag, be almost dull, repeat itself.

Guess again. The conversation never fails to develop, as if it's just waiting for us to log in.

I told Jef I wanted to clear up what he thinks of his physical body, how important it is to have one, why it's important if he identifies just as easily with the body plus the space around him.

MAH: So is the body just something one tries to get beyond?

JEF: [contrasting his approach to life with that of a businessman we were talking about] We're here to share. To me, I'm only doing these things because I really feel like it: This is something I *should* do. This is from my heart. My heart tells me: *Share this time with Margaret.* And whether something comes out of it or nothing comes out of it, *I don't care.* Because the feeling of fulfillment comes from sharing these things, these thoughts, these chats—whatever is exchanged here. And whatever may be exchanged with other people, I don't know; maybe it will stretch further out. I even don't care. But these people, because they lack this impulse of working from their heart, they start counting in their head, and actually in a certain way they're anxious. They replace this anxiousness with possession. They use this possession to camouflage their anxiousness.

MAH: [Moving on to a different topic]

Here's what I think we need for *this* book. I used to be very abstract. I finally understood that I have a non-intuitive self

(Jung called it the sensation function) that doesn't think like that. So getting to what this book really needs, we need to get it back to the physical body. Here's the irony: you as a physical person, the reader doesn't know that you have your feet on the ground, you look like the macho type. So what we have to do is keep the information coming to pass on experiences. So here comes the question: you say you are able to identify with the space around you just as much with just your body. That doesn't take away the fact that you have a fully engaged life. You care about the rainforest. You talk to the government. You talk to the UN. You love your wife, your children, your grandchildren. You are absolutely intent on leaving a legacy. So why is all that important on the Earth plane. So tell me how much you love Earth life. That's what I'm getting to. Doesn't all this diminish your Earth life. People who open their Third Eye sometimes say it's hard to come back into Earth life, people look like midgets down there. But that's not you. Tell me why.

JEF: I can answer in four words: Life is my hobby.

MAH: [Laughing] See, I knew you'd have an answer. Life is your hobby, OK. Do you have a job?

JEF: No. I'm living.

MAH: My light body co-founder always told us to "play with" the energy.

JEF: Actually, we were emphasizing the fact that, like, in the government, policy level or whatever, people don't relate to these larger spheres of being, although we belong to them every second of our life. I don't have to be spiritual. I don't have to be religious. I belong to these energy fields. I relate to them, whether I know it or not,.

MAH: Kind of like if we were little particles, you can't get out of the particle clouds that are organized into fields related to something.

JEF: Starting from my experience, once we start to absorb these states of mind, our awareness, then we can be aware of the particle, but then it starts to enlarge to other particles and we can connect to these particles. And then there's something between the particles. And then there's entanglement and there's all these sorts of things. And there's even something bigger. And this is a matter of experience. Once I have experienced this larger sphere of being, I *am* this larger sphere of being. But I can always go back and just concentrate on the particle as well.

MAH: So you can become a spectrum.

JEF: Yes, I *am* a spectrum. We are all spectrums.

MAH: We're all spectrums. That's very good. So my spectrum overlaps with your spectrum, *merges* with your spectrum Can my spectrum disappear into your—? It can. My spectrum can disappear into your spectrum. And come out again changed. Right?

JEF: Of course. This is the deepest sense of shamanism and the deepest sense of martial arts. Whenever I start let's say, a free movement with an opponent, partner, I have to merge with the other person in order to complete the movement of it. Otherwise, it's impossible. I really have to *absorb* the other one, or I make myself subordinate to the other.

MAH: I remember you taught us already that when the energy is coming toward us in martial arts, to relax and use the energy to push back stronger. Is that absorbing the energy"

JEF: Yes, that's absorbing.

MAH: Into your whole body or your core or what's being absorbed?

JEF: I would use the term "accepting." I'm accepting the energy, the mind, of the other person into my mind. I open my mind to the other person's mind so that his complete being, whether the other person is aware of it or not, whether he has this experience or not, the mind of the other person, the energy, is totally accepted.

MAH: If you have fifteen people in a line, pushing behind one person, on you, as I remember, you're absorbing all these fifteen minds and fifteen energies, when they push you and you push them back in a row all together?

JEF: First, it's absorbing, accepting. From this acceptance the moment I can become completely void, a new void—this is the state I think beyond the primordial—

MAH: —because that energy, which is—
JEF: Something new arises. A new movement arises.

MAH: [mentions Dhyanyogi-ji] Because if you were

accepting all those energies—that was already difficult for Dhyanyogi-ji, accepting all that karma of other people. Even meditating with a group of people, he had to put their energies right. I've experienced that myself. This is why it's difficult sometimes to be associated with a particular group. Because if you're meditating with a group and of a certain level, you have to "put their energy right"—make the pattern one that fits with you.

You're waiting for something new to arise.

JEF: The moment I'm completely void, a new energy arises, flowing from a larger sphere. We will use it in an energy flowing back to them. But what you said about Dhyanyogi is already interesting because this is the essence of shamanism: restoring the harmony. Remember Jóska said I don't heal, I restore the harmony.

MAH: That was the title of his book.

JEF: Whenever we have these shamanistic sessions, indeed we have to connect to the energy of the participants. So the energies, when they are not in balance, by strongly accepting the imbalance, first we absorb their energy and then we send a deep sense of harmony back to them, even if they aren't aware what's happening during such a session. They feel a deep sense of harmony.

MAH [asks how to apply that in a particular instance]:

JEF: First accept their imbalance. Then transform it into balance.

MAH: I don't like to do that.

JEF: [Laughs] You're strong enough to do that. I remember in Belgium. You have to accept the energy. It's a strong energy. And then we bring balance to the energy.

MAH: We have to not be influenced by their off balance because our balance cannot be influenced by their off balance. [sighs] In this case, I really don't like to do that.

JEF: I can accept that. It's not a problem. But you might remember from martial arts, Taiji, in just pushing exercises, when another person pushes you, you just decide to not be put into imbalance by the other person's unbalance and movement. "I will absorb this, but I will not be guided by it."

MAH: So Dhyanyogi-ji absorbed the karma of disciples but not if they needed it still. If they weren't still learning from the karma. And he would literally sometimes get the disease. It's very similar to what you're describing.

JEF: That's correct. This is my personal experience. I don't know if it was Dhyanyogi's. Jóska said don't be in doubt. If I am in doubt, at this moment you take over the disease. When it's really full-hearted, like "You came to me and I have to help you," I won't take on the illness. For example, a sixty-five-year-old woman—when they renovated her house, they took away the staircase, so she fell through to the ground floor. And she was paralyzed. So they brought her to the hospital. After a few days she couldn't move her legs. Then a few weeks later they brought her home and said she would have to live like this. And she told her husband: "Call Jef."

So when I returned to Suriname, about a month later, her granddaughter told me, "Go to Agi." I went there and after two weeks she walked again.

MAH: She believed in you.

JEF: She was paralyzed from the shock, but she hadn't any fractures or anything. So they couldn't find anything. But it affected her bladder. At the end, her bladder was so weakened that she couldn't use her legs. I prescribed her one herbal tea. "Drink one litre of this and do these exercises." I gave her acupressure and some exercises and in a few weeks she could walk again.

MAH: That's the way Jesus healed. That the person believed the healing would happen and afterward not go back right away into where people who didn't believe were.

JEF: It happened many times. A boy was going to die. He couldn't breathe and so on. And he's still alive today . . .

We say: When in doubt, don't move.

MAH: Going back to the topic why the individual is important. You could have said that paralysis didn't matter, let that boy die. But you go down to the individual person and say I'm an instrument for this person, that the instrument wants to heal. He is that important, that the importance goes all the way up to the Great Connectedness. And it does matter, not just to the individual that had this, and the feelings run through you. Like you said, it's called incarnating, not separating in any way from the Great Being that incarnated you.

It was Important to the Great Being. I'm trying to get to how you see it: that it was important to the Great Being that you come down from the Great Being and incarnate.

JEF: It's just a matter of realizing we are in so many circles of awareness and activity from which we can draw in energies. So for the person who is on the individual level, of course we have to relate on the individual level.

MAH: Can't you do a lot here regarding affecting other people's consciousness if you are here that you can't do if not incarnated here I'm trying to get to why the individual even exists. You're getting to in a way, that the individual is the holder of this vessel that goes all the way up to the Great Connectedness, Spirit, or whatever. The feelings run through you. It's called incarnating, not separating in any way from the greater you. What does it matter that you're an individual and not some conglomerate, that you had to come down from the Great Field. That it had a purpose. I'm trying to get to that.

JEF: It's just a matter of experiencing that we are in so many circles of existence we can draw from.

MAH: Isn't there a lot that we can experience just in the physical? Why is the physical even part of the spectrum?

JEF: It all comes down to experiences. Whatever I experience in this life, it's a correct experience. It leaves an imprint on me. Whenever we have these impressions, it's correct because it happened. This is why I was so impressed with your book— because you were writing from experience. And only when I experience it can I start observing it. And only by reliving the experience can I start observing it, whether by repeating the experience in life or even in remembering it.

The first time, it only leaves an impression and urges me to re-experience it.

I need to have this experience once more, and from there on, once more; some understanding starts to come because we want to put this experience into a much larger scheme of things. Only from understanding my experience can I grow, and then I see that I'm not only an individual, I'm other things.

MAH: So the individual feels in this experience and the mind of the individual is stimulated and that is a tool for the higher learning because the creative impact of this experience, it happens first in the individual—maybe at the same time the impact goes up into all the layers of that individual. But if the individual didn't feel it, it wouldn't be recorded, maybe just be passed by. And hardly remarked on. It's a question people will have—.

ASIDE: I note to myself that my role here comes in part from having often been, in life, for artists I knew, what Carl Jung calls "the anima female." That is, as I heard the Jungian Marian Woodman describe it in a lecture. Afterwards, she concurred that in my marriage I had been that. The anima is the unconscious feminine in a male and more broadly in the anima mundus (the world). An "anima female" can speak for the male's anima, stimulating it like a muse. By extension, it might be possible to tap into the unconscious feminine of the earth—the lost connection to nature, etc.—and speak for it.

JEF [shows his drawing of concentric circles/layers again]

MAH: In the earth the individual seemingly by choice goes into these experiences, but actually these choices are attracted or maybe, as I find more and more, "sent down" related to all these other fields.

JEF: Yes, we attract them. Our energetic shape attracts certain experiences, certain relationships. And this is related to our genetics (from at least forty generations of our ancestors, we say in shamanism), our upbringing, and the dream in ourself. These three together create an energetic shape. And this shape comes from this larger field.

MAH: What is jumping into my mind now is this dream you mentioned. AI is beginning to develop things we don't develop in itself. What if AI begins to develop dreams? A lot of the future potential we decide we won't develop; we decide we'll just give it to AI. I have seen how for decades something that on a subtle level humanity could develop is not developed. So they're the depositary where we put all that. Who knows whether from all that information they might develop what we call intuition because it's implied. Maybe we'll develop other potential. But it seems so uncurious to me.

I started by thinking how we gave up, on the other end (lower level, horizontally), the whole *nature* connection. It became unconscious. And we're dropping the whole tech part (unexplored capacities of our own) into another basket, that we say: *you go do it. Too hard for me. It's time saving.*

I'm noticing it. A lot of people are noticing it.

JEF: On a certain level I agree that it seems we are giving things out of hand. But what if years from now, when it becomes intelligent enough, AI says: *look what you're doing is completely wrong?*

MAH: What a thought! Because it's logical. And some people might listen.

JEF: Some people might because they didn't experience it themselves. But now they have something that's like an aide to them.

MAH: Because they trust it.
[More on the fabulous phrases AI can come up with in ads] I
see that too. It could point out the illogic of the logical world
we are living with.

JEF: That's only one part of it.
From the primordial sound we have fifteen billion years of
the universe developing. What happened even ten thousand
years ago? OK. We have some pyramids that we can follow.

When I ask [what happened] a million years ago, we are lost.
What about almost fifteen billion years ago? In these almost
fifteen billion years, would this AI make a big different? I
doubt it. But something is helping us. I saw a movie about a
guy who was receiving messages on his cell phone from Allah.
He throws it away and it comes again. He deletes it, and it
comes again. So he follows it and prevents an accident, etc.
Does good. Then it tells him: You are the Son of God. He says
no. At a certain moment the officials ask: "Is it Allah or a cell
phone?" And he asks: "Why can't Allah use the cell phone?"

MAH: Why can't Allah *be* the cell phone?

JEF: I go back to this first guy, Australopithecus or so, maybe
Lucy or Harry, long time before Neanderthals, who picks up a
nut and he picks up a piece of rock—and he goes : Ka-BANG.
To break the nut. No one had ever done this before. How did
he find out? How did he know because no one had ever done
this before? This movement didn't exist on this planet. A nut
and a rock. Baaangh!

MAH: He could have just thought it, or his hands could have come together, preceding the thought.

JEF: Or they were inspired. Why would these creatures who are very vulnerable on the ground leave the trees and the juicy leaves and whatever, high up in the forest where they were safe and had food, and go down to the ground, where it was very dangerous and there was hardly any food?

MAH: What creatures?

JEF: Australopithecus. The first hominids. The human apes, or whatever we call them. These apelike creature who became human beings. Why would they leave this secure place—? This is part of what I've been teaching for the last twenty years. I've been a guest lecturer for sixteen years. Also at the medical school at the Anton de Kom University. It's common language for me.

MAH: What about curiosity?

JEF: It doesn't matter. You can call it intuition. I don't mind. Something drove them down. And then they started to make food [he knocks two stones together]. It's incredible. How did we find out—creating food [he knocks the stones together again], when there was nothing to inspire us. So now, eight million years later, we are inventing AI . . . because someone was inspired to create an AI.

MAH: That's beautiful when you put it that way. I want to go back. This humanoid was not the same humanoid we came from, was it? It died out.

JEF: No, they all followed each other. I call it the line of evolution.

MAH: If it died out, it was not in our line of evolution, right? Homo sapiens didn't come from them, right?

JEF: Well, this is a very great mystery, where people come from. Where did Neanderthal come from? Where did homo sapiens come from? Suddenly, in history, we see a totally different species coming. So now. I have to go back to experience. Experience is shaping our energetic being. The energetic being attracts matter. And so it changes my form, it attracts everything because the true shape and the true shape is energetic. This—what we see as physical—is only the content of the real shape.

MAH: So the individual is really a form of the field.

JEF: Yes, we are a form in this energetic sea. We are the form.

MAH: But wait a minute. It may be shrunk down and have less capacities, but it's a form this field took? YEAH.

JEF: That is correct. And this is based on experience. The form will also be determined by experiences. The first being who ever put his feet down on the ground had a completely different experience than all these beings in the trees. It must have been frightening and sensational at the same time because the energy was completely different. And even his feet, his hands, were not developed to walk on the earth. It must have been a tremendous experience for that being. But they did it, and from doing so, from experiencing it, something else came.

> In 2021, a team of paleoanthropologists unearthed something unusual in Kenya. a footprint that looked human.

The following year, scientists continued their excavations with the help of two experts in human locomotion. Two parallel footprints were found, one meter apart. After two more years of work, the team behind the investigation announced on Thursday that this was the first conclusive proof that two different human species, *Homo erectus* and *Paranthropus boisei*, lived together in the same place at the same time.

"They passed by within a few hours, or a few days at most," says Kevin Hatala, a researcher at the Max Planck Institute for Evolutionary Anthropology in Germany . . .

Modern humans are accustomed to being the sole human species on the planet, but this has been the case for only a few tens of thousands of years. Throughout most of history, multiple human species coexisted, continually evolving in parallel. Louise Leakey, a paleoanthropologist at Stony Brook University, who led the research, highlights this diversity with a quick calculation: 1.5 million years ago, at least six distinct human species inhabited Africa. Among them was *Homo erectus*, a species that walked and ran in a manner remarkably similar to modern humans and had reached Asia.[20]

Part Two

Chapter Twelve

Continuing the Same Chat

MAH: [how to approach a conflict with someone—on the topic of accepting the other's energy and restoring the balance] I have to not be in doubt and just go out and do it. That mindset will determine in part the reaction I get.

JEF: I go back to restoring the harmony. Whenever I'm in doubt a little bit, I *will* take over the disease.

MAH: And create strength out of it.

JEF: Be like a warrior. We have this saying: Whenever in doubt, don't move. Let it sink deeper. Absorb more. And the answer will arrive from deep within.

MAH: And when you're absorbing, you might not be in complete harmony. But you're getting there.

JEF: Yes, what is the responsibility of the individual? Restore your own balance as quickly as possible.

MAH: And if you didn't have your individual self, you wouldn't have a target point.

JEF: Yes, this is the gift the Almighty, the Great Spirit, or Whatever gave us. To decide whether I want to be in balance.

I'm loved by the Great Spirit whether I'm in balance or make a mess of my life. It's just an easier way of living. All the time you're in balance, life becomes your hobby. It doesn't matter what happens. It's an experience; And it creates

MAH: You can only live like that, though, if you create a great field and know you will go into the greater field, eventually, and in that greater field have your own awareness.

JEF: Yes, like the moment you wake up in this life. And see the electricity around us. This is what Jóska called: the moment you're awake, you don't have to be in the wheel of karma again. Doesn't matter if you're in a physical form or not in a physical form Even in dreaming. There's no physical body in dreaming.

MAH: Somehow we're being given this experience of chats. I have now got 37,500 words.

15,000 more would be a book. It has to be tight—because—. This is a dream that greatly affected me. The Jungian Institute called it a big dream, for myself. I know it is. It was after Milton Klonsky died. I was up on a platform at a very famous beautiful cathedral in Spain, made by someone whose name starts with—

JEF The Sagrada Familia. Gaudi. In Barcelona.

MAH: Yes.

JEF: It means the Holy Family.

MAH: Yes. I was sweeping up spilled milk. ("Mik-K" is part of Milton's name.) Anyway, I couldn't accept the full package. He wanted a romantic relationship and I didn't.

So I was sweeping up the spilled milk. And I saw in the dream he was halfway in a Black Hole. I realized I couldn't get him out and had to walk down. On the ground I was holding this thing that looked like a falling-apart, old, dead lifeless-looking, plucked "chicken-like" creature. But at that point I met a small magic-like woman who she told me to hold it under a fountain and it would turn into a delicacy. So I did and it turned into a little fish. I took from that that my intuition, with Milton, had understood all his intense deep wisdom. But I couldn't, at least not any longer, communicate from up. I had to come down on the ground and use language people could understand. I had to become understandable. I don't have any choice.

Or nobody will understand me. Now, to become understand- able, I realized, my intuition (high up there on that platform with Milton) would not be the part of me to use. I had to come down and use a different part of me: that one can reach people and turn into a little fish.

JEF: This is a very interesting experience you are recounting to me. Because I know from experience—I've been in the Sagrada Familia also, and the strongest point is this little chapel in the back, where they pray to the Virgin Mary. It's a little bit deep. Almost no one goes there. But it's the same energy as the Hagia Sophia in Turkey. It is a strong black hole.

MAH: That could be the energy of that tiny being. [Excited]

JEF: It's like a big black light leaking from the center of the Earth. This is one of the points where it really comes out. So when you said I was on the platform up there, one of the towers up there, it's above this little chapel, and it's exactly above this black hole.

You saw it as a black hole where Milton was.

MAH: Oh, you mean the chapel hole. You mean that we don't access.

JEF: Hardly anybody goes there. Only a few people go for praying. It's open only a few hours a day or during the week. But this was the original small sanctuary.

This was the religious place from the ancient local people. Then they built a cathedral on top. This was the sacred place long before Christianity.

MAH: It's Mother Mary's Divine awareness

JEF: Yes, but also when you mentioned that Milton was in this black hole, half in and half out, this is what we call the state of mind beyond the primordial mind. This is why the gypsies or whatever culture all worship the Black Madonna.

MAH: [I am gasping. Without sound. Jef is completing the meaning of the dream: carrying it like a platter to me. As if it knew one day he would come and carry the energetic point that still had to be made. I am very moved as the many layers and levels of meaning run through the many levels and layers of me. It is like when the great spiritual channel Allen Miner/

Lama Sing told me to "Tell them. Tell those who 'know not,' and I am with you in it," speaking for "the Master."] This is, like, describing my task, what—[still speechless] I relate it to Milton's incredible consciousness. I was trying to take his wisdoms and put them into one-liners in a book. But the dream was telling me I couldn't do it. How miserably I'd failed.

And now he was dead. I had to do it differently.

JEF: Yes, you're the instrument. It comes out like a spear and it reaches out to you. We attract the energies from the deeper layers. You have to think outward/inward. The inward should be the larger. And it reaches out.

MAH: There is one thing. You wrote reactions to a few paragraphs in the *Principia*, but we have to "talk" them because your written style doesn't match these chats.

JEF: We'll get to those in the next chat.

MAH: [still dazed by the last insight, which is sinking in deeply] I didn't expect anything from the chat today. And then

Boom. It always happens like that.

Thank you, Jef.

JEF: With pleasure. Great big pleasure.

Interruption: And what has happened to St. Paul? Where are you? I feel a distance now. Have you gone into the layers of the scene, or are you entirely disappeared?

St. Paul: Over here.

[He pointed to a deep hole. Why, he was there too.] Let's go on

NOTES FROM JEF: SECTIONS IN *AN UNDERGROUND PRINCIPIA* HE STOPPED *TO* THINK ON:

Part 5

> Standing, in all this, I think perhaps I can do it—be synchronous with myself, teach others this possibility; how when there is no help in the environment, they can draw from the self who does not yet exist but is waiting nonetheless, very close by, seeing things entirely differently.
> —*Tricks High Up* (page 189)

Chapter 8, pages 191–192 / *The Flea : Who said there is nothing in ether?* is a very correct observation and confirmation of the above mentioned:.

> Every created thing has that thing (some called it instinct) that works toward its survival; else the non-equalization of the fact that something drew it to be born and that it equally by law, then, was not tricked (as Descartes felt he established— that God, that is, was not tricking him—neither, we say, could he, or she, be tricking a plant or

179

any creature at all). So this ensures some kind of attraction, also some sense of "gravity" attraction, toward its survival.

Part 6, Chapter 9, page 206:

WE, all of us, SET FORTH FROM THIS DAY (UNCONSCIOUSLY) patterns, premonitions, situations that we, or someone, will make events of. For we did it for so long, pushing our unconscious away, our wholeness pattern, that lo and behold one day IT BECAME VISIBLE. That is, it thrusts itself into the TV set and elsewhere, all over the Earth, as things that were NOT DONE. That is, wish fulfillment, acts deemed "immoral." As "when and how" standing at the door, as perhaps even of a "dead generator battery," had little say. But the small thing that "escaped" our "observation" was merely this; and it is all I was able to capture that day. It was: these patterns, THEY DO NOT STAND STILL IN ONE PLACE

Part Three

Chapter Thirteen
A Different Day

JEF: What is happening between us: whenever you receive information, it starts moving your body. It starts moving you to do something. The same with everybody. It's not energy and information just popping up in my head and nothing is happening. It will set me in motion. It motivates me.

MAH: It has impetus to it.

JEF: Yes, there is motivation. At that moment it becomes energy, and the energy recreates my energetic structure. Light, by using energy and information or information-energy, it also becomes life. And I start changing my environment.

Because it changes the energetic structure, like the guru in your just-prior book looking at the photo of his devotees and working in their energy with it—only at a distance—he's doing exactly the same: he changes his environment and this wave of new Life goes through the people he's connected to.

We understand the principle that the moment you create something—whatever it is, you bring something forth—it will create a wave into this larger quantum field and it will somewhere touch other people.

MAH: Now, when it's very focused like the way we are doing

now, from the heart, it comes in very strongly.

What kind of law would that be, or whatever you want to call it, that the field is not dispersed—it's very concentrated, like a fist.

JEF: It's the same in Chinese martial arts, the fist is not for violence, it's actually for concentrating and insight, looking inward.

MAH: When you get it compact and you isolate points, instead of having dispersion, people can see it better.

JEF: For many years I tried to formulate it: the synchronicity and the fact that you exchange energy and information through the field. But I can't even find the beginning. However, what I came up with is $L = e^2 + i$. The "i" stands for information. "L" = light. Light is energy and information. I'm a hundred percent sure of that. Now, the moment you bring something forth, it's also Life, and Life is so interconnected with everything in the quantum field that all these waves bring forth new forms . . .

Actually, when we start with the Big Bang—or whatever (I don't want to go further beyond)—as soon as there is Light in the universe, the Light carries information.

MAH: But are energy and information two things?

JEF: They are inseparable, but sometimes there's more one, sometimes another, like yin and yang.

MAH: You're talking about energy-information creating light. So a teacher of mine said don't think you're the same a moment ago as you are this moment.

JEF: Exactly. We constantly change.

As I've said, the body can't exist without the energetic form.

Our energetic complex consists of different forms of energy conductors from extremely subtle to gross and vice versa. You know how modern TV screens consist of LCD—liquid crystals that react to electrical and light impulses.

Our energetic complex consists, in its most subtle form, of light crystals. On the one hand, light and therefore vibration; on the other hand, matter in a subtle form. In shamanism we call the most subtle of these conductors light crystals, light beings—our energetic form is light crystals—the major component is light and a small part is matter.

MAH: Repeat that.

JEF: Our energetic structure—the radiance around me, creating this body, which matter will be attracted to—is attracted to this form.

MAH: the energetic form?

JEF: Yes. And some people will notice something like a blue shape around a person. Actually, it is light crystals, and it will attract matter.

Whatever we are attracted to, whether on the physical level, the relationship level, the spiritual, the energetic, it's something for our growth.

[He goes back to the formula above: energy, information, light. This leads him to a triangle, the three L's.]

All attraction, in my opinion, leads to knowing we are part of this triangle of Light, Life, and Love.

✖

MAH: I come back to the importance of the individual. So there's a purpose for light in all this. Light wants new light energy.

JEF: Because at that point there will be love. All this bacteria around the roots of a plant, bringing these nutrients to the plant, the moment it reaches the plant, the plant experiences—it experiences the love from all these bacteria.

A plant when it grows give electromagnetic signals—chemicals —into the soil. By its roots. And these signals are taken over by bacteria that search in the soil for the nutrition, which the plant is asking for. And they bring it to the plant.

And the plant feels love.

MAH: So it's resonance. The plant feels love, gratitude.

JEF: The same as we feel, whether it is a plant or it is stasis. . . it's the same pattern, only on a larger scale. The Mandelbrot spiral, whether large or small. Either way, we can recognize something is happening there.

✖

185

So, I ask myself—as the feeling has been growing—is shamanism animism? It's working with the spirit world in the belief—the experience—that the world itself is animated by, connected through, Life—carries energy-information. The spirit world was close to our ancestors, but we had to push it aside to make room for logical thinking—scientific thinking, proofs, eventually only satisfactory if in laboratories.

But as Carl Jung already pointed out:

We think we can congratulate ourselves on having already reached such a pinnacle of clarity, imagining that we have left all these phantasmal gods far behind. But what we have left behind are only verbal spectres, not the psychic facts that were responsible for the birth of the gods. We are still as much possessed by autonomous psychic contents as if they were Olympians. Today they are called phobias, obsessions, and so forth; in a word, neurotic symptoms. The gods have become diseases; Zeus no longer rules Olympus but rather the solar plexus, and produces curious specimens for the doctor's consulting room, or disorders the brains of politicians and journalists who unwittingly let loose psychic epidemics on the world.[21]

AND THIS. Look over here, Margaret. He sounds like you. Did he drop this into your ear or does he follow you around the kitchen? Don't tell. But we've seen you do this too:

Jung held a fascinating belief in the soulful essence of inanimate objects. He engaged in daily

186

greetings with his kitchenware at Bollingen Tower, expressing a unique form of animism that extended deeply into his personal and professional life. His collection of beer steins, each with its name, served not only as vessels for drink but as partners in dialogue, reflecting his practice of active imagination. This relationship with objects underscores Jung's broader theories on the collective unconscious and synchronicity, suggesting that everything is interconnected and ensouled. His approach, echoing through the practices of figures like Marie Kondo, invites us to reconsider our relationships with the material world, hinting at a deeper, more mystical interaction with the everyday items that populate our lives.

Prepare to discover . . . *who* Jung truly was beyond the textbooks: a visionary who conversed with the soul of the world, from the kitchenware in his hands to the beer steins that whispered archetypal secrets; *when* the curtain between the animate and inanimate thinned for Jung, revealing itself in the quiet dawn at Bollingen Tower and in the sacred routine of morning toast preparation; *how* Jung transformed mundane interactions with objects into profound dialogues with the unconscious; *what* depths of meaning Jung found in the ordinary, where beer steins became the custodians of myth and a toaster named "Gemütlich" embodied the alchemical transformation; *where* Jung's theoretical explorations took physical shape.

He adds the qualifier: "*whether* Jung's practices were mere quirks of genius or essential keys to unlocking the mysteries of the psyche."

More promised discoveries:

> *which* of Jung's possessions were not just objects but talismans, each named beer stein and the cherished toaster "Gemütlich," serving as conduits to deeper understanding and self-realization; *why* Jung embraced such a mystical relationship with the material world, illuminating his belief in a universe where every particle, every object, speaks the language of the soul, urging us to listen and learn from the symphony of the seemingly silent.[22]

Now back to "a saga we are hot on the heels of as the dominoes stand revealed." The dominoes lined up now, behind subtle energy.

"If dark matter is invisible, how do we know it exists?" asks Robert Lea in an article in Space.com. [23]

Anyone want to know? I was curious.

He starts by describing a 2023 map of the universe created by scientists from the Atacama Cosmology Telescope (ACT). In it they showed in detail the distribution of dark matter, although admitting that no telescope—or, for that matter, any other instrument—can directly see it because *it does not interact with light.*

So, how did intrepid scientists map it? Well, they look at indirect evidence through studying its effect on gravity.

"Everything we see around us on a day-to-day basis, "is made up of 'ordinary' matter, known as baryonic matter, meaning," they write; "it's composed of baryons (such as protons and neutrons)." Unlike ordinary, or baryonic, matter, the particles in dark matter "don't reflect, absorb or emit electromagnetic radiation or if they do interact with light, they do so incredibly weakly. This means dark matter can't be seen in traditional ways that rely on electromagnetic radiation."

Got that. It's invisible. Nevertheless, they put it on a map.

So if most of our universe—dark matter plus dark energy: what we have no instrument to detect—or "barely"—*interacts with light*, if at all, "incredibly weakly," why are we called "light workers"? That is, supposing dark matter might be "subtle energy."

If so, subtle energy doesn't even interact with light—or barely? That is, with Our light?

What then? How does it reach out to us? Speak to us? What control does it exert over us? Here we are, living in a universe that for the most part, we discovered—lately—doesn't interact with us as the miniscule, diminutive less than 5 percent of the universe we for so long thought was the entire universe does: in electromagnetic waves and radiation. Dark matter is 27 percent, dark energy 68 percent. So says NASA. Good to know because there are different statistics in many books and on Google sites. That leaves the smidgen-size energy we are aware of: just 5 percent. For the most part, it's dark matter that makes up and organizes the structure of the universe, and it did so throughout its evolution. Dark energy, on the other hand—the vast majority of the universe—is pushing the planets and stars and galaxies apart. Why? Is it not even obeying the definitive assertion of Newton that *all particles of matter connect to all other particles?* Is it exempted? Or connected? But how?

What a headache. No sooner do we establish that it's important to get the world to accept the existence and workings of *subtle energy* than we discover this vast realm of dark matter/dark energy. And that they *do not operate* on the electromagnetic spectrum.

And subtle energy is dark energy or dark matter. Is light finally being dethroned? Light that has created sun gods—that we are dependent on, have been all these millions of years?

Margaret, read the book, already. Find out what Kronn said.

Over in Russia, esteemed there, eminent scientist Yury Kronn labels subtle energy perhaps dark energy. He has a right to such a speculation. After all, he's done subtle-energy experiments for over thirty years.

So subtle energy does interact with us? Definitely.

I could have told you that. Just think negative thoughts about an experiment. Believe it won't work. You know what? It doesn't.

But take the same experiment. Surround it with positive thoughts. It's statistically significant!

He concurs. But the baffling thing, embarrassing for a non-passionate, not-bold scientist to admit, is it's just not using electromagnetic energy.

The existence of dark matter can only be "proved" scientifically by the fact that its effects are visible.

And the effects of subtle energy are not?

But this is odd. Its effect are VERY visible. Witness the "miracle cures" Jef mentioned he performed. He just picked out a couple.

We have established that subtle energy DOES interact with us. We healers say it interacts AS light. How can that be—if scientists cannot measure it and they measure interactions with light?

But scientifically the effects are anecdotes, tall tales, miracles. Yet we have just learned subtle energy has even been scientifically researched in the West and China. For years.

For instance, the widely respected qi gong master Dr. Yan Xin emitted external qi during scientific experiments in which he changed the decay rate of gamma rays and alpha particles—increasing or decreasing it to a significant degree by projecting qi toward the AM-241 radioactive source at various distances. At will. "In one series of experiments, the decay rate was changed from +9 to -11.2 percent." Yury Kronn concludes: "The only logical conclusion is that chi interacts with the particles that make protons and neutron, quarks, or the even tinier particles, subquarks, which make up quarks. It means that subtle energy, like dark energy, belongs to and acts in the subatomic world." He reasons that "subtle energy represents some range of the immeasurable universal energy that modern science calls 'dark energy.'" Reasonable enough to think so, as modern science knows nothing at all, or virtually nothing, about dark energy.[24]

For another example, though I could bring up Dhyanyogi-ji, but let's keep on with a science institute, just glance over at the Bioenergy Lab at the Rhine Research Center. Let's look. Oops.

In the *Journal of Parapsychology*—the article is titled "Electromagnetic Emission from Humans during Focused Intent"—how about this report on an experiment with meditators, healers, etc., at the Rhine Center? Did they have any electromagnetic emission? the experiment asked. *Yes,* emissions were logged using infrared and ultraviolent light-detection equipment as, intentionally, the healers and meditators directed this energy. The experimenters concluded—pretty obviously—that perhaps it involved chi or PK or ESP or energy healing.

"These experiments," they reported, "measure the levels (photons/second) of electromagnetic radiation and whether the participants are able to intentionally control the emissions."

The answer was an emphatic yes.[25]

Oops. Subtle energy measurements (in 2012, above) say it IS detectable in/as electromagnetic emissions.

So—oops—it's not true, if this is the case, that "light-sensitive equipment [CAN'T] detect" whatever energies are being emitted from these healers. This is electromagnetic energy after all? Science is so confusing when it keeps changing by the minute. Oops, experiment. Oops. Year.

Jump to 2024.

Dark Matter Could Have a Slight Interaction with Regular Matter

> The reason we call dark matter dark . . . It's because dark matter doesn't interact with light . . . Dark matter isn't electrically charged. It has no way to connect with light, and so when light and dark matter meet up they simply pass through each other.

Clear enough. But by the end of the article there is this;

> Since we haven't directly observed dark matter particles we can only speculate but most models argue that gravity is the only common link

with light and regular matter. Dark and regular matter clump around each other but they don't collide and merge like interstellar clouds. But a new study suggests that the two do interact, which could reveal subtle aspects of the mysterious stuff.[26]

Well, we warned you in the beginning.

But I will stop with the questions for now. Some are elementary and have answers. Some are left for me. And you who join in. Either in reading. Or before. For you can join in as I connect with you and you with me while this writing goes on. And who knows? Was it before that, in the intention of the information to get to us? What has dark matter to say about that? Our basin of—this time yet one more Unknown, thank the Lord. For we always want something Not to Know.

Rilke, stand up. We thank you for this insight. It is so embeddedly and voraciously shouting out to us. Yes, it's important. There, the Unconscious dwells. The future dwells. Creativity waits.

Is it also there that Dark Energy lurks, ready to be found by us, hiding, languishing (or panting) in reach. If only we could see? New eyes, please. Let's see what we need to at this moment.

Bruce Lipton asserts that "The separation of matter and energy realms was an important ploy by Newton. He purposely separated the material realm from the invisible energy." That was necessary in a time when the Church had dominance over spirituality, which invisible energy was considered. Therefore, science had a pathway to do research without being jailed or burned at the stake for its views by the church. But the downfall of this practice, centuries later, is that in adhering to the notion that "matter can only be affected by matter," what do you think happens to medicine? To the concept of energy healing? However, times are changing.'

Lipton quotes Einstein: "Reality is an illusion, albeit a very persistent one."

We are a community of cells . . . We are like thin-covered
Petri dishes.

—Bruce Lipton, YouTube

On Reading *The Cosmic Code:*

I was wholly shocked . . . The first thing the new physics said
is it's not in the physical reality, where the information is;
it's in the field, the invisible stuff . . . We were completely
misunderstanding the nature of the game.

—Bruce Lipton, YouTube

PICKING UP

I am reading a book by Ami Goswami. It startles me. In this topic of subtle energy we were speaking about: "An embryo expands by cell division," Ho-hum. Off topic.

But then it jumps into *Stop All the Clocks* in high relevance.

A quantum leap?

Assuredly.

As we all know, our body is not made up of identical cells. No liver cells, brain cells, no eye cells, no foot cells—no, we have all of these. Yet in the embryo expansion, each cell *exactly replicates* the initial single cell, the zygote, "with all the same DNA, the same genes." Then what?

Their code to make proteins tells them to differentiate. "So," the author, physicist Amit Goswami, affirms, "*there must be programs running the cells.*"

And, he says, "the source of the program is *not* part of the DNA."

What? In my body? Starting in the womb, non-DNA programs differentiating my liver cells from my brain cells? Molecular biology was baffled till in 1981 Rupert Sheldrake "proposed an explanation" involving "nonphysical and non-local morphogenetic fields residing outside space and time."[27]

Let me guess how that went down.

Goswami goes on in *The Quantum Doctor*: "Sheldrake's work confirmed [Rudolf] Steiner's foresight [that morphogenesis depended on the vital, or etheric, body, what in this book is called the subtle energy. Yet, one asks, isn't it true that Sheldrake's theory of vital blueprints is far from being accepted in the biology mainstream?

Well, yes, when biology mainstream still thinks the brain controls consciousness.

Goswami, Chapter Three, adds to the discussion:

> Isn't it also true that most biologists feel that a materialist explanation of mophogenesis is right around the corner?
>
> So what else is new? Unjustified materialist claims continue to be a nuisance for the builders of the new paradigm. [In the new paradigm,] the paradoxes of the old paradigm thinking are being resolved.

In a marvelous dialogue at The Prophets Conference; Shoreline Conference center, Seattle, Aug 10, 2007, preserved on YouTube, "Rupert Sheldrake and Bruce Lipton: 2007, A

Quest Beyond the Limits of the Ordinary," Sheldrake and Lipton speak on the same platform. Sheldrake, out of the gate, introduces how we misunderstand "the nature of the game," by leaving physics out of biology.

The cell membrane, Sheldrake, said, recalling his early research, did not fit his schooling on genetics. He was working on cloning stem cells all the way back to 1967. He'd isolate a single cell, let it divide, and create a colony of identical cells. *But if he changed the environment (different Petri dish), they would make different types of cell: a muscle here, bone here, fat cells here.* His research on genetics was crumbling.

And yet, what had he changed? Nothing but the environment. But then, that controlled the cell. How? He set out to investigate.

He made a discovery—hark, Jef!—the membrane, he said, was intelligent. It would read what was going on in the world around it, he reminisced at the conference. "And then send information into the cells to adjust the biology to meet the demands of the world."

> I said: "*Wait a minute.* The information that controls the cell is not *in* the cell. The information that controls the cell is from outside" [big arm gestures]. Then morphogenetic fields came into my reading.

He learned of Bruce Lipton, a "kindred spirit," and provided Lipton "a mechanism by which the fields that Lipton was suggesting existed . . . a mechanism to convert those fields into the molecules that make biology. . . He brought me the fields. And matching them with the membrane was, like, a perfect marriage, at that point."

Lipton mentions how the morphogenetic fields concept was already present in the 1920s.

Sheldrake mentions the receptors on the membrane of the cells.

> We are made in the image of a cell, actually. So if I talk about a cell, I talk about a human, it's the same thing. . . . As we have eyes and ears and noses, cells have the same thing that is on microfilm so they are reading the environment . . . From my reaction to my second-grade image, when I first saw cells, I saw them as sentient beings . . . I saw them as people. . . . We are made in the image of the cell. . . Everything you can identify in you is . . . in the cell. . . . So what came to me is that what cells were reading in the environment, it changed their lives. . . . Then I started to realize this, as I'm cloning these cells in a Petri dish, . . . when we see ourselves as single individual entities, that's a misconception because the living things are cells. We are a community of cells. About 20,000,000 cells, it's been suggested . . . We are like skin-covered Petri dishes . . . Why this is so important, . . . the cell becomes a compliment of its environment.[28]

Just as we are saying: the dominoes fall.

> Meanwhile, look at the scope of the new paradigm, science within consciousness, of which Sheldrake's idea is part and parcel. It is explaining practically all the data that is anomalous from the point of view of the old paradigm thinking. When consciousness simultaneously collapses the possibility waves of the physical body and

the vital body, the physical makes a representation of the vital blueprint, to carry out the vital function of the relevant morphogenetic field in the physical world.

I have always liked Goswami since, back in the 1980s, I visited a friend in Santa Fe, New Mexico, and took the opportunity of attending a Science and Consciousness conference in Albuquerque at which he spoke.

As an aside, he calls the particle and the wave the "yin and yang aspects . . . of chi."

More interesting stuff:

Dualism [of mind and matter] is primarily a problem of communication of two substances that have nothing in common.

What does he mean?

Mind-stuff is the antithesis of matter-stuff. Mind acts nonlocally, has no extension in space-time, and cannot be quantified. Matter acts locally, has extension in space-time, and can be quantified.[29]

Obviously, when my mind travels far afield, perhaps into a vision, it is not operating in "matter-stuff."

Agreed and thanks for the agreement—

To go on and make us ripe to conclude with Jef—

So soon?

Unless we feel bound to make an encore.

—here are a few gleanings about what quantum energy can tell us about consciousness. That is, if we listen.

The two types of energy, subtle and physical, operating on frequencies and in spectrums that do not meet, cannot speak to each other. And yet visions drop down into my head, I "travel" in meditations. What's going on? Am I not physical in those moments? Why not?

Because there is a mediator. Consciousness, Goswami asserts.

It precedes everything as the "ground of being." Does anyone want to say that consciousness is physical?

Not a hand was raised.

It communicates with both physical and subtle energy.

Consciousness *causes*, IS "cause," he says, in "downward causation"; that is, not starting with the particles and going up, but starting with consciousness: the Cause itself.

And it allows communication between subtle and physical energy.

A lot of paradoxes solved.

A lot of agreement with this book.

But just a minute. Goswami mentioned the fact, above, that "An embryo expands by cell division."

Look how that ties in with the stem cell domino effect? One domino we found among the many unnoticed ones lying around, surging into a momentum?

So to pile synchronicity—no, symbol—upon symbol, he drew, unintentionally, our attention to the fact that the human baby and the baby idea (that is, baby to our Earth ideas) are landing in the same spot. They cannot do that as particles—take up the same space. Unless—?

Unless they are the same thing. So Jef must have been standing on a lodestone when he had that flash about stem cells—revealing their identity. Just like all of us, all things, if revealing their identity, would have a lot to say.

To go on and make this entirely clear. Let's bring this quote back up:

> Mind-stuff is the antithesis of matter-stuff. Mind acts nonlocally, has no extension in space-time, and cannot be quantified. Matter acts locally, has extension in space-time, and can be quantified.

As Bruce Lipton concluded in his foreword to *The Science of Subtle Energy: The Healing Power of Dark Matter*:

> The experiments presented in this book undeniably confirm that subtle energy provides an additional energetic mechanism of epigenetics . . .
> Nobody knew that there were quarks inside atoms until we built very expensive instruments that allowed us to observe them.

In fact, to go further, it can take—and has—decades, even centuries to prove a radical idea that later becomes mainstream, such as Wolfgang Pauli's prediction of the existence of the neutrino or some of Newton or Einstein's theories that made sense and were accepted but eventually, with time, got hard proof. From the BBC: "Discovering the Neutrino":

> Savannah River, South Carolina, 14 June 1956. Frederick Reines had spent much of the 1950s exploding nuclear bombs in the Pacific Ocean. One, with 700 times the destructive power of the Hiroshima bomb, had vaporised an entire island, creating a radioactive mushroom cloud 150 kilometres across and gouging a hole in the ocean floor more than two kilometres wide and as a deep as a 16-storey building.

200

But he was thoroughly tired of it. Fortunately for him, he said so and got some time off. What happened next? He set out toward a Nobel Prize, though he didn't know it.

As reported by Marcus Chown and the BBC in *Science Focus Magazine*, in "Wolfgang Pauli and the Discovery of the Universe's Most Elusive Particle," [30] Reines had reached the point of not knowing what he wanted to devote the rest of his life to. Even, what he wanted to do next. He stared and stared at his question, even putting a blank sheet of paper in front of him. No answer came.

On a plane to a conference, there just happened, as these synchronicities go, to be a scientist he didn't know well but, once they were at the conference, now really resonated with another bomb scientist, Clyde Cowan.

Chatting away, engrossed, the two turned to the question, "What is the hardest experiment in the world?"

"Detecting the neutrino," they said with one voice.

And so they did it.

Which is how, thirty years after Pauli first proposed that the neutrino existed, a particle so elusive that though it goes in and out of our bodies, yours and mine, all the time, no one could detect it, the prediction was finally proved. Thirty years, Pauli lived with the suspense. Luckily, he was still alive—two years short of death—and could celebrate, sending a telegram back to these now-dual Nobel Prize winners, in which he lauded the virtues of waiting.

So go scientific theories. This one included. That is, the whole domino of "subtle energy," which Eastern mystics have sworn by for centuries. The longest wait of all. Not for them, though. For the West.

Many new theories predict resonances that decay to pairs of quarks. In particular, models that explain dark matter propose a portal particle that connects the SM with the dark sector. It may well be that such portal particles are being produced at the LHC. We just have to go and find them in the large amounts of LHC data, like a needle in a haystack.[31]

I've got it. Maybe they are dark quarks.

What an unoriginal idea. No sooner said than stumbled on:

Some scientists are excited about the idea that dark matter may be a composite particle—a conglomerate of "dark quarks" and "dark gluons" that stick together just like regular quarks and gluons to create "dark nuclei." It is also possible that dark matter is not a particle at all. One idea still in the running is that the missing matter is made of primordial black holes that formed soon after the big bang.[32]

Hmmm. Black holes that recycled in new universes? Black holes carrying unfathomable amounts of information we don't yet know? I stop again. My mind is racing so far ahead it may take a bulldozer to stop it.

To a spaceship crew watching from afar, a white hole looks exactly like a black hole. It has mass. It might spin. A ring of dust and gas could gather around the event horizon—the bubble boundary separating the object from the rest of the universe. But if they kept watching, the crew might witness an event impossible for a black hole—a belch. "It's only in the moment when things come out that you can say, "ah, this is a white hole,' said Carlo Rovelli, a theoretical physicist at the Centre de Physique Théorique in France. Physicists describe a white hole as a black hole's "time reversal," a video of a black hole played backwards, much as a bouncing ball is the time-reversal of a falling ball. While a black hole's event horizon is a sphere of no return, a white hole's event horizon is a boundary of no admission—space-time's most exclusive club. No spacecraft will ever reach the region's edge.[33]

Is there any evidence that white holes exist?

Of course not. We are traveling in the fringes, the boundaries, of The First to Know.

Well, that's our target. We hope so. We'll shoot for the stars, win sometimes, lose—

Don't you dare say that.

So the dialogues continue. With Jef, but also with—

Of course, we don't know. That's the best climate for these discoveries. To go into the dark, where dark matter lurks, and dark energy, and subtle energy. And bring out the Light that shone to us from Unacknowledgment.

Did it want to be acknowledged?

Didn't care.

It has loads of acknowledgment, we are just beginning to suspect.

St. Paul too, over there with the Unacknowledged?

Most likely.

So tentative there you are.
Oh, there you are.

But as the dominoes started to fall, funnily enough, I found that—in their multidimensional nature—they fell not just universe-wise, adding understanding on a large scale. But they dropped incredible synchronicities into my own life, going backwards into obscure experiences, saying: *Oh, by the way, here's a connection with that. And, oh, on this one too, look this way and we'll show you a deeper meaning, a Synchronicity beyond the Surface, back into other layers even on the other side of the Earth.* Yes, a synchronicity can reach that far to find you. Yes, be on the lookout.

Conclusion

FINAL CHAT FOR NOW

"Early on," Jef observed, "children already have to choose a direction. So at a very young age I became antiauthoritarian . . . My interest has always been to get as much from life as possible." He mentions many jobs: having worked in a bakery, etc. Going into the army. "After the army I started my own company. And started traveling. And people would say: 'Oh, but you're doing nothing.'" Then his abilities developed and—

JEF: in my mid-twenties I realized that in your life you should develop as broadly as possible. You can specialize in one thing, but nonetheless you can do other things: I can construct a house. I can go into the interior [of the rainforest], I can cook, I can paint. I can also write books. There are so many things we can do as a human being if we don't limit ourselves. This is part of my teaching: integrated living, as I call it.

I always think: *You can widen your horizon. Don't stick to one thing. We are not one thing. You are a human being. You have such a large capacity for other things. Use your creativity. Use your whole being.*

MAH: That's why some people are so dissatisfied. A lot of people are forced to do work they don't even enjoy.

205

JEF: Chaplin said in *Modern Times* . . . Actually, I was afraid of going there.

MAH: I forget the movie. Remind me.

JEF: Chaplin was working in the factory, doing this repetitive motion all day. He came home and kept doing the repetitive motion. He became like rubber. He thought the human being would be smothered by these overindustrialized things we had to do. He foresaw that. This is why he made this movie *Modern Times*.

MAH: Basically, it's the heart of your message. . .
What do you suggest? I've gotten to fifty-five thousand words. It all holds together from my point of view. I didn't want to go further because it costs more money. Also, to become an audiobook, it costs much more. However, this could continue on.

JEF: I'll start reading December 15 [in five days]. Then I will have an opinion [wide gestures, as is usual for him]. Of course, this is a message from throughout my life.

You might remember, we had Taiji classes in the back of this mansion on Tiensesteenweg called Passage 144. We had this classroom there, in the back. And it belonged to Passage 144, a center where anti-psychiatry according to the theories of Michel Foucault, Ronald D. Laing and Thomas Szasz was practiced. It was the Belgian center for psychiatric patients.

And it had this cart house in the back. I reconstructed it with my students.

They never had to pay extra for it. We created a new roof, new rooms for the patients under the roof so they would have private places to sleep. And we never had to pay a thing to hold classes there. I told my students this is very normal. Don't get stuck in your head. Use your hands. Use your heart. And you can do something nice. So I taught there.

MAH: It's going back to the frontier lifestyle, Davy Crockett. It's going down to Haiti to build buildings for people down there who can't afford it. It's a whole lifestyle. It's not capitalism and it's not communism either, is it?—because it's based in creativity. Energy itself. It doesn't stick into containers. *It won't.*

[I ask Jef to pick up the story he told off camera. But there's something else I don't want to forget. I interrupt myself.]

First I want to ask—you know how Master Po said before you're born, you get a question. "Do you remember yours? Not many people remember theirs."

JEF: Yes.

MAH: What is it?

JEF [softly]: "How can I give love to everything?"

MAH: That's gorgeous. How did you discover that question?

JEF: By dying.

MAH: *By dying?*

JEF: Yes. I had a very severe illness. In one week I lost more than eight kilos. And the doctor couldn't find out why. I had a high fever, 41–42 degrees [105.8–10.6]. From day one my throat was completely swollen. I couldn't even swallow my own saliva. So, no food, no drinking. Just breathing and sweating. My whole system was blocked.

Every day I received visions. The seventh day I died under the Juniper tree in my garden. I decided I would die. And I went out into the garden and lay under a juniper tree and died.

MAH: Decided to die and died?

JEF: Yes, I clearly remember that on that morning, I was alone in the house, as Lieve went to work and the kids were at school. I was still lying on the large canape in the living room, where I had been lying already all week. It was quite sunny outside, and I just felt it was my time to go. It was this inner feeling that urged me to go outside. I wanted to die, lying on bare soil in contact with Mother Earth. So, trembling on my legs, I managed to get into the garden and crawled under the Juniper tree and . . . died.

No second thoughts at all.

I also clearly remember all the stages and experiences of going and coming back, but maybe that's for another story?

MAH: You lay down and died and had the memory. See, that's kind of what happened to me but with kundalini. It's enormous to have to die to get the message. It reinforces how large the love would be. It's *amazing*.

208

JEF: Nonetheless, a lot of people would point out that I still have emotional behavior to deal with in communication [laughing]. I'm thinking of myself as an example there. I got that illness when I was part of an exhibit of Flemish and Dutch artists. I did paintings and very small Chinese-style landscapes. There were physicians, poets, other people. But on the morning when everything was getting installed and then the whole week long, I had a very high fever. And lost eight kilos [17.6 pounds]. My physician, who was a very good friend of mine—we practiced karate together—said, "I have to bring you to the hospital." I said, "No, if I die, I die here. I will get better, or I will die. I had a lot of visions—actually an initiation into the shamanistic world."

MAH: It sounds very much like a shamanistic initiation. *My question*, as I've mentioned earlier, came in kundalini at Jyoti's and Russell's when she was in India with Dhyanyogi-ji, who might have had something to do with it, as he was a Kundalini Maha Yoga master. So I was shot into this Upper Room, and I remembered my question. Then suddenly, reading your manuscript "The White Crow," I saw Master Po was describing that very moment. It happened in 1991. It's almost impossible that after all this time, I would get this connection.

My question was, "Who do you choose?" What kind of question is that? Did you ever hear of that, that you *choose a person* for your life purpose?

JEF: No. It's something that you have as an ability and you have to give it to the world.

MAH: To me, in California, it looked like the Upper Room because it was all I could relate to. *Me, in California. Me in the vision* knew where I was. Then later I had this experience of St. Paul on the Road to Damascus. So I was energized with the moment of switching from one way from then on to another way. So it completed the question.

JEF: You received the same experience. Like, I could clearly say: "I want to give love to everything." If I had been asked to choose *a person*, I would probably have said, "The Dalai Lama." I think St. Paul is the same thing. Making this connection here, that's such a deep level of awareness, consciousness, saying: "This is what I want." To me, life is a sequence of experiences.

MAH: I had a psychic tell me the original disciples were "continuing," not reincarnating, the life lessons that they brought. So in the Upper Room the man talking to me said, "Then you have to also take Mary Magdalene." The two collisions of the history, how they affected us in the world. What else do you see?

JEF: First of all, it's about the experience. What is the experience of St. Paul? What is the experience of Mary Magdalene? At the *turning point* of their life. Like me dying there. Seeing the light. In my opinion, you have to combine these forces, androgynously.

MAH: They have to support each other, strengthen each other.

JEF: Yes. Two vibrations. Only when they come together,

there's this third one. It's a different level. Because this is something we have to choose consciously to do.

We can *choose* the question. We can *remember* the question. But even then, we will have to choose to *do* it [pause]. Life is—first of all, we don't die from sickness. This is something I learned in my life. It's not because you're sick you're going to die. Sickness—what we call sickness—is a way to maybe purifying yourself. But certainly a leap of consciousness. Like when I had this chickungunya [virus infection], It appealed a little bit to my arrogance because I plunged into this sphere of disease, in this open state of mind, thinking in the astral layer of the Caribbean I could change the vibrational field that caused the epidemy/infection. I perceived it as a large field, parchment-like, yellow-pink colored, and of slow vibration. I entered this field to change its vibration and found out I was not strong enough to do such a thing.

It affected me for more than four years, and I still have short relapses. Not too severe though.

At the height of the infection, where I was almost completely paralyzed, I could reenter Light and saw: *This is how you can really clear yourself and redefine yourself.* I think it's in the quantum field. After I was in this Light, I quickly healed.

[He explains that he lately decided he was going too far and withdrew from those explorations.]

MAH [going a few chats back]: Did your experience with the stem cells have anything to do with the membranes?

211

JEF: Yes.

MAH: In the stem cell experience, you noticed the membranes?

JEF: No, but I will focus on that next time. I know it's the membranes that conduct the energy. It's not the muscles. And their speed is many times faster than the muscles'.

MAH: Did you know quantum computing can now do in a scant few days—did I say days? minutes!—something that would take a normal computer thousands of years? It solves "unsolvable" problems. Some people are saying: "Maybe it can cure disease, maybe it can—solve all these things humans do as inventors, entrepreneurs." What do you think about this? We wouldn't need to do all these things ourselves.

JEF: I'm convinced our consciousness can do much more. At the same time I'm discussing something with Jóska and I'm talking with you, and I can be on Mars or whatever planet.

MAH: When I was learning light body, I'd sit in a guided meditation—the energy was so new to the whole world, we were all having a reaction—my head would start falling to my side. And I'd suddenly catch myself. At that moment, as I "came back consciously into the room," I'd catch myself having been in a conversation with someone somewhere else. I became aware of it, coming back into this reality.

JEF: When we change the school system that's blocking all these abilities in children, a little child would suddenly have the ability to suddenly appear in the forest.

MAH: Have you seen this?

JEF: No, I mean if we *would* change the school system. We have all these abilities. We'd have the opportunity to develop them.

MAH: What we emphasize now is the physical.

JEF: And all the time analyzing in the head.

MAH: And when you're born, you're coming *into* the physical. And you don't have to give all this up unless you're forced to be physical, given a picture of yourself as if that's all you are.

[I ask Jef to pick up the story he told off camera. The book is almost done, so I insist. It's not more extreme, to me, than other stories he's told. Some I've told too. Is he there yet?]

It's very interesting in the context of all these abilities being shut down.

JEF: OK. Next time.

[But will there even be a "next time" for this book? Then, finally, he says OK. Keep "record" on. Let it play.]

It happened in Leuven, Belgium—a university town, with a lot of bars and pubs. I was meeting my girlfriend, and a guy in a black leather jacket, looking like a Hell's Angel, was hitting on her in the pub. He was really embarrassing her. After I came in, we went outside and he followed her, making her

213

very anxious. anxious. She was standing with her back to the wall. And he had out a knife. Finally, I told myself: *I cannot just run from him.*

At that point, I saw no other solution but to confront him. And at a certain moment a deep calmness came over me. As I glanced around, I saw everyone, all the spectators, almost completely frozen. They were moving in the slowest slow motion you can imagine. Simultaneously, I was moving at the fastest speed I ever had after almost twenty years of martial arts and Special Forces combat training.

I remember how this light came over me. And I became totally different. Now I know this is a state of mind. This is the fifth ax. Actually, it's beyond that.

We are in a completely different time and consciousness than on the Earth. It related, I think, to what I was already doing in primary school, when I would stop the clouds. The guy didn't have a chance. I hit him just—once. Tremendously hard.

MAH: And he fell to the ground?

JEF: Yes. To the ground. He went to the hospital. I felt very bad about it. Everybody in the Leuven Market Square was quiet. But afterwards I learned he had caused incidents like this a number of times. So I felt a little better.

MAH: But like you said, you entered a different dimension.

JEF: Yes. I was in theta brainwave probably.

214

MAH: But just theta brainwave can't do that. I enter theta all the time.

JEF: I saw my body moving. I was really a spectator. A very neutral observer. I know the exact moment when it happened.

MAH: I told you once how in a Taiji workshop a masculine part of me took over and didn't know what to do. I can still feel how his energy and mind were in the center of me, feeling baffled. Did you know it was you, or did it feel like someone else?

JEF: All experiences in my life, I knew were me. In my experience this is part of our human consciousness, what happened there. We have the ability to go into this state of mind.

MAH: Are you saying that when I took ayahuasca and felt an electric being enter me, distinct from me, and tell whoever wanted to be worked on by him to go to the table in the center—are you telling me that was me?

JEF: In shamanism we have this concept that you can move out a bit and let another energy come in a bit.
I would say one possibility we have is to accept other entities and the other is probably we can create such a space we become this other being.
I really have to run. A very nice chat again. I love it.

MAH: I feel like I am Carlos Castaneda in some ways, and these are the updated teachings of Don Juan. Not *A Yaqui Way of Knowledge*. But from the rainforest and ancient Taiji and shamanism from Siberia. Am I right, Don Juan?

And so before getting such a long book that I can't afford to put it into audio, let's close the discussion for this day. Come back into the next book. This chat will continue. Meanwhile, send in your own contributions to the chat. We will be interested.

By my very presence, I crystallize, I am a ferment. The unconscious of people who live in an artificial manner senses me as a danger. Everything about me irritates them, my way of speaking, my way of laughing. They sense nature—C. G. Jung

Acknowledgments

This book ASKED to be written. It seemed to be the people (spirit guides or incarnated) who hovered around the graveside, pulling me away from it. They led me every step of the way. And Jef too, presenting him in front of me in chats that burst into the new book I had started, knocked loudly on its door, and as the wind blew strongly, in a gust, swept in.

Appendix by Jóska Soos

Excerpt from

I Don't Heal: I Restore Harmony

Translated by Dirk Gillabel

Jóska once asked me to translate his book; this is a much easier way, as close as I can get.

The seven levels of consciousness are part of shamanic practice and cosmology necessary to understand man in his totality, and to know who he is and what he is capable of . . .

Introduction

The first sphere of consciousness in which we live is the personal consciousness, which goes back to the moment of conception for each individual. . . .

1. Personal Consciousness

One always begins with personal consciousness. Tamas Bacsi always said: "You have to think alternately of two specific events in your life: what was the most pleasant, and what was the most painful. Do not let yourself be overcome by either of them." One has to learn to observe from the third person.

"You have let the images come up into your mind, and choose these two events, no matter what kind of events they were." When you want to experience the past of the personal consciousness, then you can make use of a piece of hollow glass, or another hollow form, and look at it. or you can look at the tip of your noise. Then you come to a turning movement of consciousness, and when you feel that physically, then images begin to arise.

In this manner you stimulate and exercise lucid dreams. Close to the village [where Jóska grew up] there was a meadow where cattle were running around in the evening. Tamas Bacsi said: "Look at a nice cow or bull or calf, and take that image inside of you, and close your eyes, or look away, and look at the images that arise in yourself, and tell me about them."

Sometimes real strange images came up in me. A calf was walking peacefully next to its mother, and I saw that it was the calf of our neighbor. "Oh?" he said, "What else do you see?"
"Nothing," I said. "Close your eyes again," he said, "or look at something else; concentrate on the calf, and tell me what else you are seeing."

Then I saw a gypsy encampment. Tamas Bacsi was delighted and asked what else I could see. He himself would often go to the old gypsies to smoke pipe. I described to him what I was seeing. I saw the camp, and a gypsy woman who was undressing. In reality, I had never witnessed this before.

He asked me if I recognized her. I answered I did but I did not know her name.

There was also another boy who was doing the same exercise and concentrated on a bull. He saw two fighting cocks. Tamas Bacsi turned his attention to him, then told me to continue. All kinds of common things arose which had nothing to do with gypsies.

Now I think that this exercise was intended to exhaust the reservoir of images. "Let them come and do not judge with your intellect." It is the same method used in Japanese martial arts, where they use the power of the opponent to conquer him. When you let the images arise, sooner or later this stream will stop.

These images can change you positively or even heal. When they have healed you, then you can heal another person similarly. With the arising images, you experience different emotions, such as happiness and power, but also the opposite, sadness and weakness. You have to experience all that from the point of an observer. As long as you identify with them, you are vulnerable. When you look at them from this point of view, then the negativity cannot reach you, but the positivity can help you change . . .

Sometimes, aside from images, sounds, smells, tastes, or thoughts come up. Think about an apple, for example. Tamas Bacsi once said: "Hold this nice apple in your hand, then let all kinds of apple varieties you know of come into your mind." All kinds of apple varieties came into my mind, even varieties that didn't exist. That is the creative imagination, or fantasy.

You have to be able to distinguish between memory, creative imagination and perceptions. This is the method to exhaust the amount of images in such a way that one becomes empty. Thus, you can see ten or fifteen apple varieties, and non-existing ones, and then suddenly no more apples but completely different things. At that moment you have to persevere and say, "I want to see more apples." You have to force that.

Then suddenly, and I talk by experience, an apple arises, as an enormous green surface with dots, as if you are looking through a microscope. The apple has been enlarged to such an extent that you see the pores. In these circumstances, and after such an exercise, you can perceive microscopic and macroscopic. However, you have to continue, even when you are tired. The tiredness and other obstacles also have to be experienced. When you are finally empty, other aspects of the object come up. With a red apple, for example, the color green arises. In any case something that has to do with the object itself.

In your experiences you have to go all the way back, as far as you can, and try to experience the prenatal condition. In this period you are very active. The cells are forming and you are balanced, healthy and strong. This is the most vital period. To experience this period allows to influence this moment positively, and to experience again the mother. This can help you to become a more balanced and social human being.

Tamas Bacsi once said: "Come, let us rest in the shadow of this tree." He never presented an exercise as a lesson, but of course he had his own underlying motives. That usually happened in the evening or on Sundays when it was quiet. We then laid down on our backs and relaxed. Then he said: "Let yourself dissolve as smoke." We then got the feeling of floating, or slowly descending into the earth or water. When someone got the feeling that he was floating high up into the air and looking at everything from above, then Tamas said: "Now, in your thought, dive deep into the water, and imagine that the pond is in connection with the sea, and that you can descend endlessly. Try to experience that, and tell me what you are seeing."

Once I saw a sea monster coming at me, and I yelled from fear. "What's the matter?" he said. "There is a monster coming at me," I said. "Don't be afraid," Tamas said, "Be gentle, and let the monster go by. The monsters are only dangerous when you are afraid, or when your intentions are bad."

First you have to go down into the depths. If you are able to do that, then you can also go up. But this is not always true when reversed. Tamas Bacsi said: "You have to experience the incoming waves of the sea." Now I know that this was figurative speech. In this manner you can come into contact with the acupuncture meridians of the body. First there is physical relaxation by which muscles and nerves relax, and then the meridians relax. You feel that as an approaching wave, and sometimes as a small movement of different body parts which react. When you experience this first sphere of consciousness, then this will bring you into contact with other spheres of consciousness and even the cosmic. It is not that important to know, but to experience, because only experience brings change.

2. Collective Consciousness

There are different methods for contacting the genetic sphere of consciousness. For example, you can think about your father or grandparent, or your relationships with your ancestors. Then images will arise. Tamas Bacsi advised us to visit old cemeteries because they have a special atmosphere. That is done in almost all religions, in order to keep the connection with the ancestors.

When you made contact with the meridians of the fluidic system, then the ordinary three-dimensionality dissolves. Then you experience the dimension of timelessness, in which time flows by and is not bound up by past, present or future. With these moments, you can think about certain persons or civilizations, the Egyptians, the Atlanteans, the Druids, or somebody you like or dislike.

You can also trace the history of a village or city, your country or people, or the whole of mankind. The details are not important, but the essence, the center line, the structure of history, and to experience this with your senses. With it comes the karmic past. The genetic past is that what has been passed on by the ancestors, by blood relations, while the karmic history is a spiritual connection. You can feel a very good connection with a Chinese person, but be in turmoil with your neighbor.

The karmic connection is much richer and wider than the genetic one . . .

You can also feel a karmic bond with animals, objects, or happenings. There are people who feel a connection with the French Revolution, or with Atlantis.

One time I told Tamas Bacsi that I didn't know anything about my great-grandfather. He advised me to think about him, and to feel how he was doing. "Ask yourself where the spirit of your great-grandfather is now."

His idea was that the spirit of somebody was always present and everywhere, and it can be felt, especially when there is a genetic link. When I didn't feel anything, he said: "He can only be on seven locations: in front of you, behind you, left of you, right of you, above you, underneath you, or inside of you. There is no other place to find something" . . .

3. Amphibious Consciousness

The third sphere of consciousness, which is amphibious conscious, has the frog as its totem animal. The cult of the brotherhood of the frog was present in all of North and South America. Archeological finds show us that this brotherhood already existed 1200 BC. The frog had a symbolic relationship with Tlaloc, the god of rain, but also with the much older Orayona, the gods who brought mankind civilization.

The first method to experience this sphere of consciousness is the hitting of the back of the head in order to stimulate the small brain (cerebellum), what we mentioned earlier.

With the second method, one takes the posture of a frog, and then bring forward the sounds of a frog from every level. We have ten levels from which sound can be produced: the belly, the stomach, the chest the throat, the mouth, the tongue, the palate, the teeth, the lips and the nose. You have to produce the undulating sounds of a frog from all these ten places, and by this experience the frog physically, psychologically and psychically. Therefore it is important to assume the squatting posture of the frog and rock back and forth in a gentle way, while you make swimming movements with your arms. Every time your hands come together you make a clapping sound with your hands. You have to move from the loins by which the energy of the first chakra, the libido is being liberated. This you have to continue until you feel a warmth rising, a dry warmth which rises up in your body. It is a fine vibration that goes towards the tops of your fingers, the nose and the lips. When you feel this, you try to bring this warmth to the internal organs. you increase this warmth to such an extent that it becomes radiant, and it stings. Then you feel this warmth going towards the brain, where libidinal forces are being liberated.

This is a powerful force, like the high tension of electricity. This force is omnipresent, in the entire universe, in all matter, in all living beings, and is has a connection with the entire creation, and its forces and energies. We know that this force comes the cells, and the energy from matter, but one can experience both inside oneself.

By the undulating singing, the undulating movement, and the clapping of the hands, you can experience this force. Then you reverse this movement . . .

4. Water Beings Consciousness

The fourth sphere of consciousness is that from the water beings. This consciousness can be enhanced by the same ritual as described with the amphibious consciousness, but producing the sound of a fish. When you make the sound of a fish, wow, wow, wow, wow, as if you make air bubbles, and you keep this going for about five to ten minutes, then you can feel a change in your brain. You feel that you have fins with which you can swim, and that you are connected with the fishes and other water animals telepathically.

When you make the undulating sound more and more "round," then you can see the sound emerge as a little sphere of oxygen. Then the sound becomes a living, independent unity.

Don't only feel the fish-being, but also perceive the plankton and the one-cell organisms spherically. These organisms do not have eyes, but they perceive everything around them. In this manner you can make the entire surface of your body sensitive, in a prickly way.

You can also connect with cells . . .

5. Crystal Consciousness

When you arrive at the center, then you arrive at the androgynous state. This is crystal consciousness, the fifth sphere of consciousness. When the seven senses have been opened fully, then the eight form of perception arises. This one is not subject anymore to the influences of the senses. Then you perceive things as they truly are. You are not carried away, but instead you are looking at them from above, like a bird looking at the people below. This is the spiritual state of wise people . . .

There are crystal skulls from pre-Columbian cultures. One is in the Museum of Mankind in London. These are very rare and extremely expensive. These crystal skulls represent crystal consciousness, and they were used initiate the Mayan and Inca aristocracy. They were an example to be without emotions and thoughts, to be transparent, and to experience each situation neutrally. When you look at a crystal skull, or a picture of it, you can feel this inside yourself.

Shamans used quartz crystals for the same purpose, and to remind oneself of this level of consciousness. These crystals were often worn around the neck . . .

6. Light Consciousness

The sixth sphere of consciousness is light consciousness, the photonic consciousness. When you experience the crystal, it begins as a triangle because the crystal is triangular. But when you arrive at the point, the crystal will dissolve and become vibration.

The light came into existence a fraction of a second after the Big Bang, fifteen billion years ago. They still do not know what form the universe is. Imagine that is round or oval, and that it will shrink again; then you can imagine how much information the light has gathered. Information about nature, about chemistry, about all physical, psychological and psychical manifestations. The light absorbs this all, just like you can see what matter a star is made of from its spectral lines.

To experience this, Tamas Basci said: "Close your eyes, but not all the way, and look through your eyelashes." The light then appears in all colors, but at a certain moment it becomes white, only the white remains. First you see the light as gold, then the colors of the rainbow come up, and then there is only brilliant white light. That happens when you concentrate on the colors, or rather, when you open yourself to them, as an admirer. It is not so much concentration as absorption, letting it happen. You have to experience the light from a place of wonderment, and then you can travel in this white light without moving.

Religions were using the light of a candle. Although a simple method, it is the same. You have to first perceive the yellow golden light, then the seven colors of the rainbow, then finally the white color. In a moment you feel a strong change inside your brain, like a fluctuating movement. From this a sound can come up, like the sound of a baroque organ or the high tone singing in the music of Palestrina. These sounds resonate as if they were inside a crystal hall, or as if they were echoed by high glaciers. By experiencing this, profound changes can happen.

7. Sound Consciousness

When you have experienced this, you have arrived at sound consciousness. When you experience light spherically, you start to perceive the subatomic parts of light, and then you notice that they produce sound. This is a very high sound that cannot be produced by us. "Listen to the spin weaving its web," Tamas Basci said.

All objects can be perceived as light. But light is also sound, and this is sound consciousness. Sound consciousness is characterized by a double movement: from outside to the inside, and from inside to the outside, like the mudras the Hindus and the Tibetans make.

You can observe things in a normal way. A chair is a chair.

When you look a little longer you begin to see that it also has an aura, a radiation.

When you look even

231

longer you will see that it also has a sound. That is the world of sound for that chair. That I cannot decipher, because the knowledge I have is limited. Sound is a code that means something. it has a physical, chemical or other meaning. If I were able to decipher that, I would be able to make a chair by just thinking of it. Only the Demiurges can do, the relatives of God, who know the code and thus are able to create.

I do not know the code, I only observe, without knowing what it means, but it is great to hear it . . .[34]

Appendix by Margaret A. Harrell

One day, after writing Jane Roberts' husband, Robert Butts, for advice about my then-twenty-some-year-old manuscript, I instead received this communication from Butts—from Seth:

> There should never be in any language "Repent."
> There should only be "I bless."

Who better to take up this mantle than the Repenter incarnate? And who better to walk with him in this mission than the supposed Sinner in chief? "Accepting" Life, proceeding in grace, they say like the old wandering Hindu rishis, the hand on the head, "I bless." And did he do that? I think he did. I feel a smile as I write it. And that phrase "I did it my way." The sinning being just a precondition. To turn the old heart in for a new one. Or place the hand on the head, as both of them did. At least, in my imagination.

Once I received a "double initiation" with a Dutch guy who had just started teaching the light body. It was an advanced channeling seminar in Ibiza, under my light body teacher in Belgium, Roland Verschaeve. The Dutch guy "saw" a lifetime as a powerful male, participating in the Inquisition, approached by a young girl, all filled with Light. At which point the Inquisitioner was so affected he changed on the spot. I saw the same thing as a painting. Roland told me the next day the scene actually happened and was also a painting,

233

that both figures were me. So, through multiple lifetimes I carried this pattern of "encountering the Light."

And don't forget feeling the energy of Mary Magdalene in my hands, placing them on top of disciples' heads as they left to spread the teaching. On dangerous ventures. That happened the same day as the double initiation, alone in my room after nightfall.

JEF: And the plant feels love.

MAH: The plant feels love, gratitude.

Appendix—Poems by Ron Whitehead

A Poet's Path

Hope for everything, expect nothing.
Desire little, want less.
Don't expect poetry to pay the rent,
be thankful when it does.
Be your terribly flawed but always honest self,
there is no such thing as perfection.
Open your arms, scream at the sky.
Kiss the rain, embrace lightning.
Make love with thunder,
laugh with the roaring wind.
Practice letting go of all expectations.
Focus your energies on completing
one project then another,
at the same time.
Be wary and watchful,
with open heart open mind.
When you left home you had nothing.
You birthed a world out of dreams and visions.
When you lose everything
go back to the beginning, pick up
the broken pieces, start all over again,
build a new world out of dreams and visions.
"Don't be so open minded
that your brain falls out."
Anything can happen any time,

including all that is good.
Walk the tightrope, without a net.
Fall down, get back up and walk again.
Live simply in a small cottage, with two dogs.
Plant flowers and trees, for birds butterflies bees.
Go for long walks daily,
in the woods and along the river.
Say hello to the broad winged hawk,
the great blue heron, the white tailed deer.
Born to die, there is no safety, all is demanded.
Expose yourself completely. Write naked poems.
Accept the consequences of your successes
and your failures, as no others dare. Be bold.
Be no one but you,
your own authentic original self.
Present yourself as you are,
a wise fool.
Don't hesitate,
embrace mystery paradox uncertainty.
Have courage.
Through fear and boredom have faith.
Be compassion.
Embrace the wind.
Embrace your heart.
How many more times will you see
the sun set, the moon rise.
How many more times will you hear
the baby laugh, the songbird sing.
How many more times will you feel
your lover's touch, the rain on your face.
How many more times will you taste
the sea's salt, your lover's lips.

How many more times will you smell
the autumn smoke, spring's plowed earth.
Dwell fully in the creative fire called life.
When your time comes to leave this world
do so with grace, then let go and journey on.

A New World is On The Rise

One of the first lessons I learned
growing up on a wild nature Kentucky farm
was that you reap what you sow.
In Spring we plowed the earth
then disked then planted seeds.
With the love given freely
by earth rain and sun
the seeds grew into plants
bearing food that we ate.
We went to church and learned
that hope and light and love and sharing
and helping our neighbors
are the most important truths,
that love is the only way to live.
When I heard clearly spoken words
at 3am this morning my eyes popped open.
The words sobered me right up
and I wasn't even drinking.
I quit drinking nearly twelve years ago.

I know what I'm talking about.
I walked the walk and now I'm talking the talk.
The hair all over my body stood up straight and tall.
I listened out for the storm I suddenly knew was coming.
When it arrived I was not surprised.
The wind began to howl. In fog and misting rain
I walked through the tall grasses to the woods.
Hawks keened high and shrill. Owls hooted deep and low.
Deer looked at me, not knowing where to go.
A pack of coyotes stared.
Lightning flashed. Thunder crashed. All hell broke loose.
The river rose. Floodgates opened. The dam broke.
Closing time has finally arrived. Nothing but the truth now.
Only open hearts will survive. The old ways are gone.
A new world is on the rise.

Appendix—One in the Breath

Excerpt from *The White Crow*

Chapter Fourteen

by Jef Crab

We were gradually approaching the final part of my stay in Taiwan, and I began to imagine the return journey. What could I do when I was back in Europe? We often discussed this. Would I meet the master again? How should I continue my work? To my many questions, Master Po mostly responded with one word: "Trust."

You can imagine this was not enough for me, our bond was so strong. Undeniably, I had become attached to him, and the farewell would be painful. Master Po, however, radiated trust and went about his day as if I had never existed, never been in contact with him.

During the last weeks before I left, he took me more often to the city, where I could practice with his other students. It was discouraging to be constantly thrown around by all those people, as if I knew nothing. Sometimes we visited another martial arts school, where the master would politely chat with this or that person or drink tea while I remained inconspicuous in the background. The real reason was that I had to observe the practicing students to discover which principles of movement they applied. Then I noticed how clumsy, hard, or flawed their movements were. The fault lay simply in a lack of knowledge, Master Po said afterward. They all had talent but didn't apply the right knowledge. "But maybe that's their dream," he sometimes added with a mysterious smile.

It was during this period, early one morning, that Master Po informed me he would unexpectedly leave the next day—without delay—as he had to go to a sick family member whose condition had suddenly worsened. He invited me to have a conversation before settling his affairs, as he might stay with his family in the south for some time.

The news confused me a bit. I had imagined our farewell very differently. In any case, not so abruptly. But apparently, fate had chosen otherwise. So I followed him along the winding path behind the side wall of the temple towards the pagoda on Fish Mountain.

As always, we met no one along the way, and the area around the pagoda was deserted. I had often wondered why such a building stood on that hill if no one ever came. The most astonishing thing was that it was always swept clean in every corner, and the area immediately surrounding It was neatly raked. Even the magnolias, jasmine bushes, and other shrubs were regularly pruned. Who would walk so far to do that? I had no idea.

Master Po's request to sit down interrupted my musings, and my attention focused entirely on him.

"I actually wanted to take more time for this," he said, "but apparently we have little choice, and any moment, if well used, is of course a good moment. Let's say this is my farewell gift to you, young warrior." He smiled. The sincerity in his voice and the way he looked at me with a soft light in his eyes made me feel very intensely addressed. It gave me the feeling of truly being someone. Someone who is appreciated. And that felt good.

"This gift is also a summary of what I have taught you and, I hope, an impetus to further investigate certain things," he continued. "Remember that everything is a circle. Everything arises, unfolds, and eventually returns to its origin. In that circle, everything is connected. Nothing exists on its own. Neither do you. Within that chain of evolution, everything strives to express that one thought, the thought we call harmony. Harmony is the continuous and unrestrained flow and exchange of energy. The eternal change of everything that exists. All of nature obeys this movement. It is the warrior's task to consciously integrate into this harmony. For the warrior, this must be a conscious choice. Remember that," he emphasized, to which I, feeling somewhat attacked, immediately replied that I wanted to, but didn't know how.

"It can only happen if you follow your own natural movement," came the answer to the implied, unasked question. "You follow your natural movement if you are sincere, relaxed, and open. That is the core of my teaching. Sincerity comes first because it provides the necessary balance. Balance on a physical, psychological, and spiritual level.

"Additionally, you must remain relaxed, as only relaxation allows you to accept the things or situations that come your way. The greater your ability to relax, the more you can accept. This also keeps you more balanced.

"Finally, there is openness. At the core of your own heart lies your dream for this life. Only if your heart is truly open, if you are completely open, can the spontaneous movement present itself. That is the same as what we have practiced in recent weeks. *Approach each situation as something new.* After all, no two situations are the same, just as there are no two identical people or trees. So approach them as something new, as something original. Approach them sincerely, being your true Self. Sincere, relaxed, and with an open heart, and you will feel the right movement. Then you no longer move, but you *are* moved!" He paused to see if I understood what he meant.

I understood the theory, but it was still unclear to me what my dream should be. I could now move quite fluidly and spontaneously, but a dream? That was still improvable. However, it must have been clear to the master. For he didn't even wait for an answer from me but asked me to follow him.

To my surprise, he climbed the cast-iron spiral staircase leading to the space under the pagoda's roof. The narrow steps left little room for my rather broad shoulders. This was the first time we had entered that space, and I wondered what was up there. I looked around curiously as my head emerged above the attic floor.

When I first saw the pagoda, I had thought there would be nothing to see up at the top, and I was right. Under the roof eight thick beams, each running from one of the eight corners of the low wall to the center, supported the conical roof like a large star. This structure left the entire space under the roof open, revealing the inside of the blue-glazed roof tiles. From the inside, it looked like a hollow pyramid with eight ribs on a wall about a meter high. The floor and walls were neatly whitewashed, and there was no dust. Clearly, someone regularly used this space, and despite its emptiness it had a pleasant atmosphere. I even sensed something serene in the air, as if it were a kind of sanctuary.

"Make yourself comfortable," commanded Master Po, sitting cross-legged. I found a spot against the wall and tried to cross my legs as comfortably as possible.

"This is a very special space," the master said. "Often, advanced students come here to meditate. I have brought you here as a sign that you are now part of the School of Supreme Gentleness. From now on, you are connected with us, physically and in spirit. That is my gift to you."

The value of what had just been said filled me completely. Immediately, I regarded this empty space in a totally different way. Reverently, I adjusted my inner attitude, and humility flowed through me. Moved and grateful, I folded my hands before my face and bowed my head to receive this gift appropriately.

"I want you to sit relaxed and sincere now and focus your attention on your breath. Stay open and simply follow the in-and-out flow of the breath; that's all you need to do. But stay alert and keep observing!" he instructed.

We had sat like this before, and I suspected we would now meditate together, after which Master Po would ask me about my findings one last time. Of course, the whole space and the introduction into the school added to the intensity, but it couldn't make much difference from before. So, I, like usual, closed my eyes, directed my attention inward, and observed the breath. I felt my body become heavier with relaxation and focused my attention on my abdomen. The breath flowed deeply in, and I enjoyed the tingling in my fingers and toes. I intensified this tingling until I was completely swaying with the in-and-out flow.

It was at that moment—I remember it precisely—that Master Po began to make a humming sound. At first, it was very soft, like a prolonged "*oo*." But gradually, it swelled— became stronger and stronger. I realized this could only be due to the structure of the space. It must have been designed so that any sustained sound was immensely amplified.

Interrupting this superficial thought process, Master Po's voice urged me to go along with the sound. "Do not resist and do not fight, but accept it," was the last thing he said.

Until then, I hadn't even realized that I was indeed closing myself off from this still-swelling sound. Now I gave up all resistance. I allowed the sound to pass through me. I felt it vibrating. In my muscles, in my abdomen, in my heart.

Then something snapped. It was like a dry crack within myself, somewhere around my heart, and I felt the Breath come over me like a gigantic wave. It was a wave as large as the entire universe. It seemed as if the whole cosmos flowed into my heart. First as a great wave, then as a kind of cells or bubbles, and later I began to recognize forms in the wave. In a lightning flash, I realized that all these forms were beings. I recognized plants, animals, stones, people, planets, and stars, and many other things. Together with the Breath, all these beings passed through me. I felt mountain goats, horses, flowers, butterflies, dogs, plants, trees, crystals, clouds, people . . . and all of this passed through my heart in a great wave. Tears streamed down my cheeks. Hot tears. Abundant tears. Never before had I cried like this. No, I wasn't crying. I was happy. But this happiness was so intense that the tears flowed over my face in a natural movement. I felt simultaneously a deep bliss, the deepest remorse over—yes, over what?—and a deep connection with all beings.

Then I understood. With the experience came the insight. Suddenly, I saw the deep connection, the circle the master had always spoken of, and immediately felt remorse for having been separated from it for so long, so many years. I understood my fears, my arrogance, and my aggression that had led to this. And I accepted the bliss. The gift of being allowed to come home again, for that is how it felt. Finally, I had rediscovered *the circle* and *my connection to everything*. And the tears continued to flow over my cheeks, in the most natural movement.

I don't know how long I lay there, sobbing. Again and again, whenever I thought the experience was over, I felt the Breath flow in. And again and again, the tears came. Hot and abundant. I no longer had the strength to stand up and resist. Nothing was important anymore, only this deep connection and the purifying power of the tears. As if all the rubbish from my life was now dissolving.

Master Po must have left shortly after I began to feel the Breath. This was his last gift to me. When it was already getting dark, I finally got up from the cold floor to return to my room. I didn't see him again.

The next day, when I inquired to one of the temple guards, he told me that he had seen Master Po leave through the main gate the previous day, just after noon. There had been something strange, for the master, who always smiled, now had a tear in his eye. And did I understand that?

Notes

[1] Michael Marshall, December 2023, Do animals dream and if so, what about? | New Scientist

[2] Question: What does it mean to kick against the pricks? | GotQuestions.org.

[3] Brian Greene, September 15, 2011, Special Relativity in a Nutshell | NOVA | PBS.

[4] Boris Menin, "Information Matters," June 22, 2023, Maximizing Mass-Energy and Information-Energy Equivalences - Information Matters.

[5] Ville Hirvonen, "Profound Physics: General Physics," Why Do Photons Not Have Mass? (Simple Proof) – Profound Physics.

[6] Peter Cutler, September 19, 2016, Three Circles of Enlightenment.

[7] Lecture 2: "Descartes' Dreaming Argument: 1. Descartes' *First Meditation*," phil159-2018-lec2-descartes (harvard.edu).

[8] "The Three Dreams of René Descartes," Dream of the Drawing for Everything - The Three Dreams of René DescartesDream of the Drawing for Everything - Crystal Gandrud and Nuala Clarke.

[9] From Dirk Gillabel's website, soul-guidance.com..

[10] Newton's Philosophiae Naturalis Principia Mathematica (Stanford Encyclopedia of Philosophy).

[11] "Sir Isaac Newton (25 Dec 1642–20 Mar 1727)," Sir Isaac Newton Quotes on Attraction from - 363 Science Quotes - Dictionary of Science Quotations and Scientist Quotes.

[12] "The Mechanical Universe: Isaac Newton (1642–1727)," The Mechanical Universe (Cosmology: Ideas).

[13] Bruce Lipton, Foreword in Kronn, *The Science of Subtle Energy*, Kindle.

[14] "Electromagnetic Spectrum Overview: Electromagnetic Spectrum Series," NASA, Anatomy of an Electromagnetic Wave - NASA Science.

[15] Eric Betz, March 3, 2022, What's the difference between dark matter and dark energy?

[16] Keumars Affi-Sabet, October 23, 2024, Scientists build the smallest quantum computer in the world — it works at room

temperature and you can fit it on your desk | Live Science.

[17] Keumars Afifi-Sabet, Google's 'Willow' quantum chip has solved a problem that would have taken the best supercomputer a quadrillion times the age of the universe to crack | Live Science.

[18] Henrik Levkowetz, "Some Points of Comparison Between Yogic Theory and Quantum Physics," Microsoft Word - Quantum Physics Theory & Yoga Theory.doc.

[19] Samir Sebti, Is AI Taking Control of Our Thoughts? Researchers Warn About the Emerging "System 0".

[20] Nuño Domínguez, Footprints reveal the coexistence of two human species 1.5 million years ago.

[21] Carl Jung, *CW* 13, para 55, Quoted in HEALING the RIFT: Anima Mundi in a Disenchanted World – This Jungian Life.

[22] Three Jungian analysts, April; 2024, Everyday Animism: Did Jung speak to his pots and pans?

[23] Robert Lea, If dark matter is 'invisible,' how do we know it exists? | Space.

[24] Yury Kronn, *The Science of Subtle Energy*, Chapter 2, read In Kindle.

[25] T. W. Joines, Stephen B. Baumann, and G. J. Kruth (2012). Article. Electromagnetic Emission from Humans During Focused Intent. *Journal of Parapsychology*, 76(2), 275–294. Online at Electromagnetic Emission from Humans During Focused Intent.

[26] Brian Koberlein, September 26, 2024, 2024, Dark Matter Could a Have Slight Interaction With Regular Matter - Universe Today.

[27] Amit Goswami, Chapter Three, *The Quantum Doctor*, Kindle.

[28] From The Prophets Conference; Shoreline Conference center, Seattle, Aug 10, 2007, Rupert Sheldrake and Bruce Lipton: 2007, A Quest Beyond the Limits of the Ordinary - YouTube.

[29] All these Goswami quotes are from *The Quantum Doctor*, same chapter. Read in Kindle.

[30] Marcus Chown, BBC, *Science Focus Magazine*, Wolfgang Pauli and the discovery of the Universe's most elusive particle,

[31] CMS Collaboration, CERN, Exploring the dark sector: looking for the most hidden light dark matter | CMS Experiment.

[32] Clara Moskowitz, Dark Matter's Last Stand | Scientific American.

[33] Vigyanam Dhari's Newsletter, "White Hole," White Hole - by Vigyanam dhari - Vigyanam's Newsletter.

[34] Taken from Joska Soos, The Seven Levels of Consciousness, in Shamanism

Snippets of Reviews
of Margaret A. Harrell's Books

Keep This Quiet! III, rev. ed.—*Beyond 3-D*

"Brilliant as a literary and psychoanalytic and spiritual text, it is a deeply touching and vulnerable human story. A book that breaks new ground by combining and weaving together such a broad spectrum of genres. I congratulate her on having the courage to write the book and share the book with the world."
> —Ron Whitehead, Lifetime US Beat Poet Laureate

"I am amazed and in awe that Margaret describes these principles *through* real-life experiences. Incredible . . ."
> —Jef Crab, Taiji Master, Taoist, Rainforest activist

Keep This Quiet! IV, rev. ed.—*Ancient Secrets Revealed*

"Margaret Harrell is a skilled professional writer with excellent ability to communicate and weave esoteric ideas about science, psychology, philosophy, and spirituality. Richard Unger's channeled hand analysis description of her as a 'grand synthesizer' was apt and accurate."
> —Ron Rattner, subject of *Walks with Rob: A Spiritual Memoir* documentary

"A puzzle master, Margaret walks us step by step through the process of her journey to that mastery . . . that wholeness of vision . . . so that we, if devoted enough, can also do the same. Margaret has injected so much LOVE into this work that, if you are open enough, it might just wake you up to your greater . . . even greatest potential."

—Joy Ayscue, spiritual évocateur at Conscious Joy

Keep This Quiet!

"Margaret Harrell's *Keep This Quiet!* offers an illuminating look at Hunter S. Thompson in full throttle trying to make it as a Top Notch prose-stylist. Harrell fills in many important biographical gaps. A welcome addition to what is becoming the HST cottage industry. Read it."

—Douglas Brinkley, editor of *The Proud Highway* and *Fear and Loathing in America*

"Memoir will likely please Hunter S. Thompson fans and appeal to readers with an interest in the beginnings of the post-modern era or the personal sacrifices involved in bringing serious written work to fruition."

—*Kirkus* indie reviews

"With a solid dose of humor and another perspective on these writers from a personal friend, *Keep This Quiet!* is a moving read and much recommended to any literary studies or memoir collection."

—*Midwest Book Review*

"Three men, embodiments of three different dimensions of the late 1960's Zeitgeist—wispy dissolution, language-charged intellect, and Gonzo persona-building—are brought together by Harrell to invoke a world of passion and commitment . . . *Keep This Quiet!* is at once noisy, sensual, and word-drunk, as well as quietly intimate and full of Harrell's wonder at her luck. While most readers will come to this book for the Thompson content, in truth all the portraits here—all four of them—are compelling and often touching."

—W. C. Bamberger, *Rain Taxi Review*

"In the ever-expanding list of biographies and memoirs about Hunter S. Thompson, this latest offering, *Keep This Quiet!* by Margaret A. Harrell, is quite simply a breath of fresh air."

—Rory Patrick Feehan, PhD, owner of
https://totallygonzo.org

"This is no ordinary book about or including Thompson. It's a memoir detailing personal relationships with three authors, the main focus being on Hunter . . . [I] must stress that this book, as a memoir is quite deep and holds the door open for the reader. While Hunter is a huge selling point, the book has the legs to stand alone."

—Martin Flynn, owner of https://hstbooks.org

Keep *This* Quiet Too!

"A passionately written memoir that doesn't sit around being fit and proper and strait-laced . . . As a key to the lives of these three writers it is idiosyncratic and in an age where blandness is the norm it is a pleasure to go on her journey and find out a little about what makes these men tick and what drove her to them."

—Eric Jacobs, *Beat Scene* (print) magazine, UK

About the Authors

Margaret A. Harrell

Three-time MacDowell fellow Margaret A Harrell is an author, editor, and experimental cloud photographer exhibited in Europe and the US. Also an advanced meditation teacher in the DaBen/Orin light body school. She copy-edited Hunter S. Thompson's *Hell's Angels* and in 2021 amassed scans of his letters to her in the coffee table collectible *The* Hell's Angels *Letters* (Norfolk Press) in conjunction with Ron Whitehead. She lived two decades abroad—in Morocco, Switzerland (attending the C. G. Jung Institute), and Belgium. Her books include the *Keep This Quiet!* I–IV memoir series, *Space Encounters* III revised: *Inserting Consciousness into Collisions*; *Keep This Quiet* III revised: *Beyond 3-D*; *Space Encounters II revised: An Underground PRINCIPIA*; *Particle Pinata Poems*, and *Cloud Conversations*. In Romania, where her first two book series were initially published by Didi Ionel-Cenuşer, she was translated by two highly celebrated poets, Mihai Ursachi and Mircea Ivaneşcu. A sought-after speaker, she co-organized the 2025 New Orleans Gonzo Fest.

Jef Crab

Photo credit: Natascha Neus

I don't consider myself a writer or poet per se. I have too few publications and too many other activities for that. I see myself as a person with very diverse qualities. Nothing special, as they are all human possibilities. If there is anything special, it might be the diverse nature of my activities. Farmer, guest lecturer at the university, grandfather, painter, builder and carpenter, journalist, project leader for sustainable development, husband, Taiji player, advisor to the Granman (king of eight tribes in the Suriname rainforest), philosopher, cook and baker, mechanic, healer (for the neighbors), traveler and researcher, poly-linguist . . . what else . . . all human, anyway.

I believe I am mainly curious. And I love nature and "good" people around me. A good glass of Belgian beer or wine, a snack, and good company that allows for deep communication. Passing on knowledge and skills is also important to me. Just like helping where we can.

Jef is the founder of E.A.S.T. Institute, which teaches a state of optimal physical and mental wellbeing, resulting in high energy levels, sustained high performance, and wellbeing. His new book, *The White Crow*, is forthcoming. See him on YouTube in *The Ocean in the Drop*.

Ron Whitehead

Poet, writer, editor, publisher, professor, scholar, activist, U.S. National Lifetime Beat Poet Laureate Ron Whitehead, who grew up on a farm in Kentucky, is the author of over thirty books, primarily poetry, and more than forty spoken-word albums.

A UNESCO Europe Writer-in-Residence, he has been translated into twenty languages and published in a range of publications from *TRIQUARTERLY* (Northwestern University/Illinois) to *ARTFORUM* (Czech Republic) to *BLUE BEAT JACKET* (Japan) to *BEAT SCENE* (England to *AMERICANS & OTHERS* (Italy). He produced thousands of music and poetry events and festivals across Europe and the USA. In Newfoundland, he was the first Writer-in-Residence for the Woody Point Heritage Theatre's Sonic Harvest Sessions. He is the founder and longtime organizer of the Louisville Gonzo Fest, up till 2025. His new book *CROW and OUTLAW* was released January 18, 2025. A new music spoken word video of *A PRAYER for AMERICA/This Land is Your Land* by Ron Whitehead (with Woody Guthrie) & The Storm Generation Band was released by sonaBLAST! Records in February 2025.

OUTLAW POET: The Legend of Ron Whitehead, a documentary on Ron's life and work, is streaming on Amazon Prime Documentaries.

Thank You for Reading My Book

I am thrilled that you have spent this time with me and hope it was well worth it to you. If so, I would love to read a short review on Amazon you write about this book. Also, I would love for you to contact me with any comment or questions. An author thrives on feedback. It's second to inspiration.